CPR for
NONPROFITS

CPR for NONPROFITS

Creative Strategies for

Successful Fundraising, Marketing,

Communications, and Management

ALVIN H. REISS

JOSSEY-BASS
A Wiley Company
San Francisco

Jossey-Bass books and products are available through most bookstores. To contact Jossey-Bass directly, call (888) 378-2537, fax to (800) 605-2665, or visit our website at www.josseybass.com.

Substantial discounts on bulk quantities of Jossey-Bass books are available to corporations, professional associations, and other organizations. For details and discount information, contact the special sales department at Jossey-Bass.

Manufactured in the United States of America on Lyons Falls Turin Book. This paper is acid-free and 100 percent totally chlorine-free.

Library of Congress Cataloging-in-Publication Data

Reiss, Alvin H.
    CPR for nonprofits: creative strategies for successful fundraising, marketing, communications, and management/Alvin H. Reiss.—1st ed.
      p. cm.—(The Jossey-Bass nonprofit and public management series)
    Includes bibliographical references.
    ISBN 0-7879-5241-9 (acid-free paper)
    1. Fund raising—United States. 2. Nonprofit organizations—United States—Finance. 3. Nonprofit organizations—United States—Management. I. Title. II. Series
HG177.5.U6 R45   2000
658'.048—dc21

00-010233

PB Printing 10 9 8 7 6 5 4 3 2 1   FIRST EDITION

CONTENTS

CHAPTER THREE: Asking for Money   77

CHAPTER FOUR: Involving Your Board and Reaching Your Audiences   109

CHAPTER FIVE: Pursuing the Corporate Dollar   139

To Ethan, Josh, and James Reiss, my now and my future

PREFACE

SEVERAL YEARS AGO at the conclusion of a speech before a conference of cultural administrators, I was asked by one of the participants to indicate just what it is that I enjoy most about my work. Barely pausing to consider my answer, I responded quickly, "The possibility of the unexpected." What I was saying wasn't unique or especially revealing. I was merely reveling in the fact that because my work doesn't involve a set routine—although obviously there are routine aspects to it—there are many times that interesting and exciting things happen, seemingly out of the blue. It could be a call inviting me to undertake a lecture tour or a letter asking me to participate in a key study in a special area of my interest.

Some time later, reflecting on my response, I realized that as involved as I am with what I do, and as exhilarated as I am from the exciting things that result from my work, nothing really ever happens out of the blue. To use the vernacular of baseball, the invitation that seems to "come from left field" has actually resulted from "my time at bat." Something I have done at some point in my work life triggers a response down the line, often very far down the line.

The nonprofit organizations that I worked with to complete this book clearly had some very good times at bat. The dedicated and capable individuals in these groups, involved in a wide range of fields and activities, not only have responded successfully to ongoing challenges but also have triggered in some instances what might seem (to the uninitiated) the unlikely result—the giant grant from someone who had never given such a large amount before or the expansion of the organization's audience to include a new and sought-after constituency. For them, the seemingly unexpected happened because of the professional way in which they approach their everyday concerns.

In seeking out these kinds of organizations and trying to identify the activities that best illustrate their good times at bat, I have not been concerned with size or scope. What has been important is the concept. This becomes evident by looking at some of the cases. There is the example of the university that won an $80 million bequest from a donor whose largest previous gift had been $4 million. Along with it is the case of the theater company that won considerably less—three $1 million gifts. Those gifts, however, were all received in a short period of time and were the first gifts of over $1 million *ever* won by the theater.

Similarly, although it's a given that a nonprofit's national advertising campaign that promoted its message to millions of people and won numerous awards would be deemed an unqualified success, how might another campaign that was designed to win only a small number of positive responses be viewed? In the context of this book, if the latter campaign met its specific goal by developing a successful plan to attract the small number that it sought, then it too would be judged a success. Hence the case of a giant national organization is presented along with the case of a small suburban library that broke new ground by developing and introducing a program that succeeded, for the first time, in involving fathers in a Saturday afternoon parent-child program.

In a prior book, *Cash In! Funding and Promoting the Arts,* I introduced a phrase that I've since used over and over again in my work—*adapt, don't adopt.* I think that it is worth repeating here, for this is the message I hope to convey. The cases presented in this book have not been selected because of a particular organization's scope of operations or prestige. Nor have they been chosen solely because of the spectacular success of a particular venture. Although success in achieving a goal has been a key factor in selection, it has been equally important to find those instances in which the concepts used by the organizations have been best suited to meeting a particular need. It is the concept, then, that is adaptable; and even if great similarities exist in the kinds of challenges cited, each pathway leading to a positive result must be adapted to the specific needs and circumstances of an organization. Of course, every case will not have immediate application for every kind of nonprofit organization, but there should be enough cases that will arouse interest and challenge readers to relate them to their own circumstances.

There is one other point worth stressing. Although this book focuses on institutions and the challenges they have successfully met, it is the people in these institutions, both the professionals and the volunteers, who have been able to move the institutions from challenge through plan and ultimately to a positive result—my *CPR*. The nonprofit field has grown incredibly over the years, and it has had a positive impact on virtually every area of society, thanks to the passion and professionalism of the people in it. The health, social action, educational, cultural, religious, and other organizations whose cases have been selected for illustration, as well as the individuals who lead them, represent what has become the norm in nonprofit management—excellence and professionalism. The contributions of the entire industry have made this book possible. They have also made it an imperative for this writer to undertake.

New York, New York   Alvin H. Reiss
July 2000

ACKNOWLEDGMENTS

AS THE 1990s drew to a close, I called Jossey-Bass and spoke to associate editor Dorothy Hearst about a proposed writing project that I thought might interest her company. Although the book I had in mind didn't quite fit Jossey-Bass's publishing needs, she enthusiastically suggested that perhaps we should explore other book concepts. After many conversations with Dorothy, a frequent exchange of materials, and one delightful luncheon, this book resulted. Looking back, I know that this book could not have developed in the way that it has were it not for Dorothy's insights and constructive suggestions and her warm encouragement on virtually every step of my difficult path. I am grateful for her help and support. My thanks go also to Dorothy's associate Johanna Vondeling, who has been helpful in many ways in finalizing my manuscript for publication.

Finally, I would be remiss if I didn't express my gratitude to the many dedicated administrators I spoke to, frequently at length and often at times when they were facing program and funding deadlines, in putting together the cases that follow. Virtually without exception, they gave me the information I needed, when I needed it, in spite of their busy schedules. This book is their story, and they deserve not only my thanks but also the continued support of all the audiences they serve so well with their programs.

A.H.R.

THE AUTHOR

ALVIN H. REISS has played a pioneering role in the arts and other nonprofit areas as an educator, author, consultant, and program innovator. He is the editor and publisher of *Arts Management,* America's first journal for arts administrators, which he founded with Alvin Toffler in 1962. He is director of the Professional Arts Management Institute and founder of and coordinator at Marymount Manhattan College's Arts Management Certificate Program. Since 1985, he has been the "On the Arts" columnist for *Fund Raising Management* magazine.

Reiss lectures and consults frequently throughout the world and has presented lecture tours and residencies of one to two weeks in Japan, Australia, Romania, British Columbia, and several U.S. states. As the QEII Arts Council's Distinguished Visitor, he conducted a sixteen-day lecture tour of New Zealand in 1994. He has addressed international conferences in Spain, Austria, Canada, and the United States and has presented seminars on arts funding, marketing, corporate sponsorship, and tourism in numerous cities, including Hong Kong, Vienna, St. Croix, Copenhagen, and Stockholm.

Reiss founded and directed a graduate arts management program at Adelphi University for eight years. He served as visiting professor of arts administration at the Philadelphia College of the Arts and as visiting fellow to the graduate arts management program at the American University.

The author of hundreds of magazine articles on the arts and on travel for both consumer and cultural periodicals, as well as many studies and reports on arts issues for both cultural and business organizations, Reiss also has written humorous articles for such periodicals as *Esquire,* the *New York Times, Playbill,* and *Diversion.* His six previous books include *Culture and Company, Cash In! Funding and Promoting the Arts,* and *Don't Just Applaud, Send Money.*

He is winner of the Austrian Business League's International Management Club Award for his activities in the arts; and in 1986, he was recipient of the Outstanding Achievement Award of the International Society of Performing Arts Administrators for "exceptional service to the performing arts as innovator, author, publisher, and educator."

CHAPTER ONE

Getting Your Message Heard

BEFORE A NONPROFIT organization can reach out for support, it must first define its mission and focus on ways to communicate that mission to the publics it serves and to the other audiences it wishes to reach. The ability to communicate then is not just necessary, it is essential.

The primary role of communications for a nonprofit organization is to articulate clearly why the organization exists and what needs it must meet to fulfill its mission. Another, ongoing role of communications is to focus on specific issues as they arise and promote day-to-day organizational activities. The cases presented in this chapter represent a microcosm of the wide range of communications concerns facing nonprofits of every type and size. They include finding a way to use the media to reach millions, using a trusted voice to articulate a message of concern, promoting a concept or event, issuing dramatic evidence to bolster a key contention, and even counteracting inaccurate or incomplete information.

Despite the overt differences, there is a thread of commonality running through all of these cases. Each of the organizations crafted a carefully considered and artfully developed approach that was on target in meeting a major challenge. In some instances, words were the weapon of choice; in others, visual images were used to articulate a message with drama and fervor. In every instance, what stands out most is the organization's awareness of the scope of the need to be met and its diligence in finding the best way to communicate that need.

A Tearful Reminder

Developing Potent Messages That Articulate Your Case

BACKGROUND

Keep America Beautiful was founded in 1953 to promote litter prevention and community beautification efforts. Supported by several hundred leading American companies, it developed, over the years, a national network of hundreds of community organizations and statewide affiliates and the annual grassroots involvement of several million volunteers.

○ CHALLENGE

Nearly two decades after its founding, the organization had made a positive impression on the public through its many public service announcements and programs. Yet despite the organization's growth as a public awareness program and the ongoing support of many major corporations, many Americans still had not heeded its message. Clearly, there was a need to develop a simple yet effective way of impressing Americans with the warning that we were despoiling America with our litter.

◐ PLAN

The beneficiary in 1971 of a pro bono promotional campaign under the aegis of the Advertising Council, Keep America Beautiful turned to the agency assigned to the account, Marsteller, in New York City, to come up with a clear and dramatic means of conveying its message. After studying the problem, the agency recognized the importance of addressing not only the issue of debris litter but also the entire question of pollution. Marsteller convinced Keep America Beautiful to take the approach of alerting the nation to the dangers of pollution. Recognizing that perhaps more than any other group Native Americans agonized over the pollution of America's resources, Marsteller cast Iron Eyes Cody, a Native American actor who had appeared in many movies and was personally committed to environmental causes, to appear in the spot. Cody agreed after he was assured that the campaign would indeed be part of a long-term effort to save the environment. The resulting public service spot featured Cody paddling in a canoe down a river polluted with oil slicks and physical debris and then passing an industrial complex spewing pollution into the air. It then shifted to a scene of Cody standing on a highway as a car passed and a passenger threw refuse out of its window. As the bag of garbage broke at his feet, an agonized Cody shed a tear. The tag line for the PSA read, "People start pollution. People can stop it."

● RESULT

The spot received its first public airing on Earth Day in 1971. Used in television and transformed to print media and billboards, the Crying Indian campaign was a dramatic, impact-making alert to millions of people on the

Crying Indian photograph from Keep America Beautiful Campaign.
Reprinted with permission of Keep America Beautiful, Inc.

dangers of pollution. In time, it became one of the most effective ads ever used by a nonprofit organization to get its message across. The impact was so great in fact that the ad was voted one of the fifty top commercials in broadcast history by *Entertainment Weekly* and won a number of Clio Awards for the ad agency that produced it, Marsteller. The message was so effective that even after its run ended, it couldn't remain in retirement for long. In 1998, on the twenty-eighth anniversary celebration of Earth Day, Keep America Beautiful revived the image of Iron Eyes Cody shedding a tear for new and perhaps even larger audiences. A new "back-by-popular-neglect" campaign featured a thirty-second television spot, showing the original image of Cody, this time in a bus shelter, shedding his tear as people boarding a bus left litter strewn behind them. In addition to the thousands of airings of the PSA, its rebirth triggered major news and feature stories on network television and in metropolitan newspapers. The tremendous impact of the commercial can be gleaned from the fact that a special April 1999 issue of *Advertising Age,* "The Advertising Century," cited Keep America Beautiful's Crying Indian as number fifty of the nation's top hundred advertising campaigns of the century. Several months later, in an America Online poll, several hundred thousand subscribers who were asked to list their favorite commercial from among the ten listed cited the Crying Indian as their all-time favorite.

QUESTIONS TO ASK

1. If you're working with an ad agency, either volunteer or pro bono, have you given the firm the license to turn its creative juices on?

2. If your campaign has proved to be effective, have you, in a positive sense, developed means to exploit it?

3. Have you looked at ways to sustain the momentum that an effective message helped create?

LESSONS LEARNED

Heed the advice of professionals when you solicit it, and if a concept works, don't be afraid to use it again.

LAST WORD

A single image can create many lasting impressions.

In Him We Trust

Leveraging Key Relationships

BACKGROUND

In July 1994, a small group of religious leaders came together in Washington, D.C., to express concern over the growing power of the religious right and (as they saw it) its manipulation of faith and politics. Their meeting ended with the formation of a new organization, the Interfaith Alliance, charged with promoting the positive, healing role of religion in life while challenging all forms of what they perceived to be religious political extremism. To complement the political activities of the organization, a public education and research arm, the Interfaith Alliance Foundation, was established the following year.

○ CHALLENGE

The alliance grew steadily over the following years, attracting new members and support. Yet recognizing an urgent need for increased backing to allow it to undertake key programs to challenge the messages that religious extremists were sending to millions of people, the alliance investigated ways to significantly expand its membership. Two stumbling blocks were evident: the alliance didn't have the finances to launch a giant direct-mail campaign, and it didn't have a respected nationally known figure to sign a letter to potential members. When the direct-mail firm A. B. Data agreed to provide some initial seed money and to help with a mailing, a membership package was prepared and sent over the signature of board chair, Albert Pennybacker. The mailing was effective and helped raise alliance membership from virtually zero to about twenty thousand. With a momentum developed, the alliance, recognizing an opportunity, knew that the time was ripe for it to take its membership drive to an even higher plateau.

◑ PLAN

To realize its potential, the alliance decided to develop a national advisory board. Through organizational connections, it was able to attract a number of well-known figures, including Terry Anderson, who agreed to serve as chair. Anderson was the Associated Press journalist who was held hostage in Lebanon from 1985–1991, longer than any other American. In planning for a new mailing, organization leaders knew that if they could attract someone with the stature of Walter Cronkite, widely recognized as one of America's most trusted figures, to lend his support to the campaign, it would really make a difference. Anderson put the alliance in touch with Cronkite, and conversations with the television commentator followed. A number of options were explored, including designating him as honorary chair, before Cronkite, impressed with the organization and its message, agreed to sign a letter endorsing the alliance.

● RESULT

In January 1997, the alliance commenced its new direct-mail drive, with Cronkite's signed letter—the outside envelope bore his name as the sender—as the cornerstone of the campaign. In reviewing the draft sent to him in advance, Cronkite made only one small change, removing a postscript. The mailings—consisting of the Cronkite letter, a flier about the alliance, a letter from an alliance leader, and a reply card and envelope—have continued regularly since then. To emphasize the alliance stand, the reply card, listing donation boxes of $25 and higher, was headed, "Dear Walter." The text read, "Yes! I want to take a stand and help the Interfaith Alliance say 'NO' to Pat Robertson, Ralph Reed and their fellow extremists." The direct-mail acquisition letter, sent to over 4.6 million individuals between January 1997 and May 1999, drew a return of about 1.4 percent and attracted over seventy thousand new supporters to the coalition. It also won a major marketing award for A. B. Data. Perhaps equally important has been the relationship that the alliance has been able to build with Cronkite. Alliance leaders have kept in touch with him regularly, reporting on organizational progress and sending him snippets from the letters they receive from new members. In 1998, the alliance announced the creation of the Walter Cronkite Faith and Freedom Award to honor individuals sharing the values of the alliance. Cronkite attended the announcement kickoff press conference. In addition, Cronkite has agreed to participate in a video project endorsing the alliance stand against religious political extremism. As one alliance staff member said, "We're lucky to have Walter Cronkite involved with us. He's made the major difference."

QUESTIONS TO ASK

1. If you've developed a relationship with a nationally known figure, have you found ways to strengthen that relationship by keeping that person informed of your organization's progress every step of the way?

2. Have you offered options to that person for further involvement?

3. Have you publicly thanked that person for his or her involvement?

LESSONS LEARNED

A key public figure can lend credibility to your mission. If you do not have access to a national figure, then a respected leader of your community may serve you well.

LAST WORD

Engender trust in your cause. It is possible that nothing will be as important to you.

The Power of the Press

Launching Effective Advocacy Campaigns

BACKGROUND

Greenpeace was founded in 1971 by conservationists who believed that verbal protests were not an effective way to register serious concern about assaults on the environment. Through nonviolent, although sometimes provocative, tactics, this multinational organization with over five hundred thousand members has carried out numerous protests, often attracting worldwide attention, against threats to endangered species, the dumping of toxic waste, nuclear testing, and other key areas of concern.

○ CHALLENGE

Among its many issues of concern, Greenpeace targeted the genetic alteration of crops. Beginning some years ago overseas, and since 1996 in the United States, Greenpeace has tried to identify products that because of genetic alteration might prove harmful to consumers. It hoped to find ways to get the manufacturers to discontinue making these products. Greenpeace did not target food companies specifically; but as the technology of genetic alteration continued to develop, it became evident by 1999 that the food industry, and specifically the makers of baby food, should be scrutinized. With sufficient evidence of alteration, Greenpeace could then organize and conduct an all-out advocacy campaign to alert the nation to what it saw as a growing danger.

◑ PLAN

Greenpeace decided that its essential first step was to determine specifically which companies and which products were involved in alteration. Greenpeace staff bought a wide range of baby food products and sent them to an independent laboratory for testing. Greenpeace then sent questionnaires to every one of the eight companies—including industry giants, Gerber, Heinz, and Beech-Nut—whose products were purchased and asked them a range of questions regarding their policies on using genetically altered ingredients. Only one company, a small one, responded to the questionnaire, indicating that it never had and never would genetically alter any of its products. When the independent laboratory report indicated that a three-grain cereal made by Gerber, Gerber Mixed Cereal for Baby, and two nutritional supplements made by medical food producers were genetically altered, Greenpeace decided it was a call to action. A press conference was called in New York on June 18, 1999. Greenpeace officials, joined by Martha Herbert, a distinguished neurologist, and Aisha Ikranmuddin of Mothers & Others for a Livable Planet, discussed the findings of the laboratory report and the response to their questionnaire—or lack of response—from baby food makers.

● RESULT

Although press conference attendance was sparse, enough positive developments came out of it to make a difference. The CBS national news filmed part of it and reported on genetic alteration without mentioning Gerber; however, a story in the *Los Angeles Times* on the conference day included findings of the laboratory study on the Gerber and the other products using genetically altered ingredients. With national attention drawn to the issue, and faced with calls from concerned consumers questioning its position, Gerber announced about a month after the press conference that henceforth it would not use genetically altered ingredients in any of its products. A front page story in the *Wall Street Journal* summed up the impressive Greenpeace victory. Headlined "Strained Peace, Gerber Baby Food, Grilled by Greenpeace, Plans Swift Overhaul," it indicated that Gerber was going even further than Greenpeace had demanded by using organic corn and soy flour and that another company, Healthy Times Natural Foods, had switched from canola oil, which in some cases is genetically altered, to safflower oil because of Greenpeace's efforts.

QUESTIONS TO ASK

1. Before beginning a specific advocacy campaign, have you done your homework and come up with the facts?

2. Have you given your potential adversaries a chance to respond before you go public?

3. Have you determined the best way to launch your effort, and have you found allies to join with you and help broaden the case?

LESSONS LEARNED

Advocacy for your cause should be an ongoing effort. If you have a specific cause beyond your overall mission, make sure that you gather all the information you will need, find respected allies, and develop a plan to take your case to the publics you wish to reach.

LAST WORD

Public opinion is a powerful weapon, and by harnessing it, even a David can confront a Goliath and perhaps slay him in the process.

I've Heard That Song Before

Reinforcing Familiar Images

BACKGROUND

Since 1990, Housing Works, in New York City, has provided housing, support services, and advocacy for homeless men, women, and children living with AIDS and HIV. Its activities have been supported by proceeds from its Used Book Café and from the sale of merchandise donated to its three Housing Works Thrift Shops in Manhattan, each offering quality designer merchandise at low prices.

○ CHALLENGE

For approximately a decade, the Housing Works Thrift Shops have been doing two mailings a year, spring and fall, soliciting donations of furniture, clothing, housewares, and other items. Looking for a way to arouse interest and reach more people, Bill Gover, director of the stores, was able to prevail on a friend, Michael Ian Kaye, a top designer of book jackets, to contribute a motif for the thrift shop trucks that pick up donated merchandise. The truck design, in orange, blue, and yellow, with a message urging prospective donors to contribute merchandise, was introduced in 1998. It attracted so much attention that Housing Works, which tries to use a different design for its mailings each season, decided that the truck design was worth adapting to other uses.

◑ PLAN

The motif used on the sides of the trucks was transferred to oversized postcards, which featured the locations and phone numbers of each of the thrift shops on the address side against a plain white background. On the reverse side, a message designed to engage the reader's attention was outlined against a bright orange background, beginning, "Warning: This card may cause you to donate your sofa, your lamp, your pants, your raincoat, your records." Interspersed among the more than forty items mentioned were key phrases, highlighted in yellow, such as "your desire," "your heart," "your support," and "your compassion."

● RESULT

Between April and June 1999, some three hundred thousand cards were mailed to a list of prospective contributors. According to Gover, the mailing was a tremendous success. It resulted in one of the largest—if not the largest—responses ever, so large in fact, that additional space had to be found to house all the donated items. As an indication of the mailing's success, many people mentioned the card specifically when calling for a pickup.

QUESTIONS TO ASK

1. Before deciding on the message or approach you'll use for a major mailing, have you looked at everything you already do to see if any of these concepts are adaptable?

2. As visual identity is important, have you searched for an image that can clearly and unmistakably focus on your organization and its message?

Warning: This card may cause you to donate your sofa, your lamp, your pants, your raincoat, your records, your desire, your chair, your pots, your blender, your heart, your shoes, your ring, your suit, your care, your toaster, your coffee cup, your trust, your watch, your cereal bowls, your clock, your scarf, your garden tools, your earrings, your help, your soap dish, your belt, your vision, your answering machine, your baskets, your pans, your napkin holder, your bracelet, your support, your dishes, your t-shirt, your microwave, your radio, your forks, your skirt, your hat, your desk, your sweater, your awareness, your telephone, your spoons, your jacket, your slippers, your saucer, your rug, your teapot, your compassion...
Thank you. Housing Works Thrift Shops

Housing Works Thrift Shops mailing card. Michael Ian Kaye, designer. Reprinted with permission.

3. Have you sought artistic or design talent to help you develop a visual identity symbol?

LESSONS LEARNED

Visual identification can be a powerful force that focuses recurring attention on an organization. Before spending your energy on developing new visual symbols, look carefully at what you've already done to see if some symbol or symbols might be adapted to new uses.

LAST WORD

Familiarity breeds contentment.

Gorillas in Your Midst

Developing Market Strategies to Kick Off New Activities

BACKGROUND

The Bronx Zoo, which opened in 1899, is the largest urban zoo in the United States. Officially designated the Wildlife Conservation Society, the zoo covers more than 265 acres and features 6,000 animals and 665 different species. With over two million visitors a year, it is the top family attraction in New York City.

○ CHALLENGE

The zoo was preparing for the June 1999 debut of one of the most innovative and ambitious exhibits it had ever undertaken. The Congo Gorilla Forest, four years in the making, simulates an African rainforest and is designed in such a way that after experiencing it, visitors become keenly aware of the need to support the conservation of the rainforest and its inhabitants. Planners knew that the exhibit, with its two troops of gorillas, would attract tremendous attention, but they had been having concerns that the public's awareness of the zoo and its recall of the zoo's advertising were down slightly, indicating a need for a major marketing and advertising strategy.

● PLAN

An advertising strategy was developed to focus on the opening of the Congo Gorilla Forest, with specific emphasis on the eight weekends following the pre-opening festivities. The target audience for the campaign was identified as women between twenty-four and forty-nine years old with children between two and eleven, living within a seventy-five-mile radius of New York City. It was decided that because of the news value of the opening and the photogenic attraction of the exhibit, television would be a prime medium to use during the kick-off phase. To support key weekends, television would be supplemented by a series of print ads with a decidedly light touch for placement in major newspapers. Ads in suburban papers would be placed during the summer. To create excitement around the exhibit, pre- and postopening special events with promotional value but little cost were added to the overall marketing mix.

● RESULT

The launching of the Congo Gorilla Forest was a critical, promotional, and monetary success, boosted by tremendous press coverage. The print ads, showing gorillas and other animals that were included in the exhibit, were designed to attract attention through their low-key humorous messages, with such headlines as "Gorillas in Your Midst" and "Rookie of the Year," which featured a juvenile lowland gorilla. One of the ads that featured animals read, "Please check all pockets for pygmy marmosets before leaving Congo." Another read, "The rock python hunts by sensing body heat. Hopefully, that chill running down your spine'll throw him off." Additional marketing support came from an eight-weekend sponsorship by State

Farm Insurance, which added advertising and promotional dollars to the campaign. Among the attention-getting weekend events was a group of over twenty traditional African artists—musicians, drummers, and stilt walkers among them—parading through the African exhibit. Other events included face painting, which transformed youngsters into Congo animals, and an African mask-making program for children. The advertising and the promotions paid off. Overall attendance at the zoo in the four months following the opening increased by 7 percent. Equally significant was the fact that admission charges for the special exhibit and some additional donations during the same period raised over $700,000 toward a key goal of the exhibit, conservation of the African rainforest.

QUESTIONS TO ASK

1. In developing a marketing campaign to boost a special program, have you been able to target the precise audience you wish to reach?

2. Has your advertising captured the special and unique flavor of the program or event you're promoting?

3. Have you integrated all aspects of a campaign for its maximum impact?

LESSONS LEARNED

A successful marketing strategy is much more than a single activity. A strategy must pinpoint its target audiences, find the specific media to reach them, and present its message in such a way that each audience it reaches remembers the message.

LAST WORD

A light touch is often the right touch.

Cost Efficiency

Financing Major Promotional Campaigns with Pro Bono Support

BACKGROUND

San Diego is home to a number of major performing arts groups as well as a growing number of smaller music, dance, and theater organizations. A service organization, the San Diego Performing Arts League, has been promoting its activities to potential audiences since its founding in 1983 through such ongoing efforts as a regular newsletter, a calendar of events, a discount ticket booth, and an annual Bargain Arts Day, at which patrons are told to "pay what you can afford" for tickets offered by any of the 130 groups affiliated with the league.

○ CHALLENGE

Over the years, the league has done a more-than-creditable promotional job. Its leaders felt, however, that there were still pockets of the population that were not being reached. Clearly, there was a need to make a unique effort to significantly raise the level of awareness of the performing arts in San Diego County.

PLAN

With insufficient funds on hand to embark on an all-out promotional campaign, but not wishing to downgrade and compromise what it envisioned as a giant effort, the league decided to see if it could finesse a campaign using as much volunteer support and contributed space as it could muster. With this in mind, the league presented its board with a concept built around four key goals—to significantly raise awareness of the performing arts; to position them as fun, affordable, enriching, and valuable; to drive ticket buyers to performing arts programs; and to drive ticket buyers to league programs. The board, which includes representatives of member arts organizations and the community, agreed on the importance of the effort; and as a demonstration of their commitment to the project, individual board members contributed $10,000 in seed money to fund the creative design that would jump-start the campaign. With the help of the local chapter of the American Marketing Association, the league was able to win the pro bono services of one of San Diego's top agencies, Di Zinno Thompson Integrated Marketing Services, to create a campaign that the league hoped would elevate the status of the performing arts in San Diego. The league also wanted the campaign to be local, unique, beckoning, and fun and to make attendance at performing arts events a "cool" experience. The creative team at the agency jumped at the opportunity to donate its services because it gave them a chance to show off their promotional skills in the kind of campaign with which they might not otherwise be involved.

● RESULT

The open-ended campaign, over two years in preparation, featured billboards, print ads, bus shelter posters, PSAs for radio and television, broadcast promotions, and the design of a Web site, all with the same tag line, "San Diego's Performing Arts. Come for a Change of Scenery." The five print ads, all fun oriented and featuring local performers, included one showing a ballerina, with the line below it reading, "There's a little artist inside of everyone. We just let ours come out and play." The league itself, along with many of its member organizations, integrated the campaign into its marketing materials. Community groups picked up the campaign as well, with such contributions as free ads in nine media outlets, inclusion in the Convention and Visitors Bureau Visitor Pocket Guide, the pro bono design of the league Web site, an advertising direct-mail package sent to fifty thousand homes, and promotion on airport vans. To increase visibility for one of the key print ads, the league was able to convince the San Diego Symphony, a member group, to feature the ad on its big-screen "jumbotron" during one of its concerts. In addition, the league began soliciting local businesses to underwrite different aspects of the campaign, which resulted in sponsorship donations. By late 1999, six months after the April 1 launching of the campaign, thousands of dollars worth of donated advertising had been generated, along with what league marketing director, Toni Robbin, claimed was "fantastic publicity." Because it was difficult to quantify the results of the campaign in audience terms, the league planned to add a fulfillment element, an incentive premium, to be able to track results. Early in 2000, the league had its Web site redesigned to include the six images featured in the campaign. It also redesigned its performing arts guide to include a different campaign image in each issue of the bimonthly guide published during the year. Thanks to the positive response, the league still had not spent the $10,000 donated by its board members even many months after the campaign's launching.

There's a little artist
inside of everyone.
We just let ours come out and play.

MUSICDANCETHEATRELIFE

SAN DIEGO'S PERFORMING ARTS   COME FOR A CHANGE OF SCENERY

619.497.5000
www.sandiegoperforms.com

1999 SAN DIEGO PERFORMING ARTS LEAGUE

San Diego Performing Arts League print ad. Courtesy of San Diego
Performing Arts League/Beauchamp Studios.

CPR for Nonprofits

QUESTIONS TO ASK

1. Have you carefully determined what message it is that you wish to convey?

2. Have you developed a list of businesses in the community that might benefit by donating their services to your organization?

3. Have you presented a plan to your board and your constituents to show why you should undertake a major promotional effort, and have you solicited their support?

LESSONS LEARNED

There may be all kinds of pro bono help available to you, if you know who to ask and what to ask for.

LAST WORD

You don't have to spend a lot of money to make your point.

The *Times* Is Hard

When Good Publicity Isn't Good Enough

BACKGROUND

In 1992, families and friends of several children afflicted with Canavan disease, an illness that afflicts Jewish people from an Eastern European Ashkenazi background, joined together to form the Canavan Foundation. A key foundation activity was the support of research that would lead to the development of accurate carrier and prenatal tests for the disease. Once those tests were developed, the foundation would then educate the medical and the target populations about the disease and the existence of the tests. In the following years, as the genes were identified and accurate carrier and prenatal tests were developed for the primary target population, the foundation, while continuing to support research, stepped up its campaign to emphasize disease prevention. It embarked on an education program that included mailings to rabbis, public service announcements, advertising, and information through its own Web site.

○ CHALLENGE

For nonprofit causes seeking to broadcast their case to potential supporters, a detailed article about their concerns in the *New York Times Magazine* would fit anyone's bill of a major public relations coup. In anticipation of just such an article, the Canavan Foundation mailed its annual appeal letter shortly before the article was due to appear, alerting their supporters to the upcoming story. But when Canavan Foundation leaders first read the story, "Keeping Jacob Alive," about one family's struggle to deal with Canavan disease, in the December 6, 1998, issue of the *New York Times Magazine,* they were upset. The article failed to tell the entire story about the disease, which they thought had to be told. Although the article was compelling and called national attention to the horrors of this illness, it did not report on a key point relevant to dealing with Canavan disease—that reliable carrier screening existed to prevent the disease from occurring. This lapse, organization leaders agreed, had to be bridged.

◐ PLAN

Within two days following the article's appearance, the parents of Morgan Gelblum, the seven-year-old girl who died in 1997 from the disease (the mother, Orren Gelblum, is president of the Canavan Foundation), sent a letter to the editor at the *Times,* praising the handling of the story by the writers but indicating that the article "did not make clear a crucial fact: this kind of tragedy could have been avoided and never has to happen again."

The foundation board waited two weeks, hopeful that the letter would appear in the newspaper. When it didn't, they decided that their concern about the article's major omission had to be voiced, especially because supporters had been alerted in advance to the article's appearance. On December 20, the board sent the Gelblum letter, with a cover letter explaining the situation, to its entire mailing list of eighteen hundred supporters.

RESULT

Gelblum and several board members received a few phone calls thanking them for the letter. Although donations continued to arrive, it was difficult to determine if they resulted from the letter. Yet despite the less-than-hoped-for response, the board recognized at its next meeting that the magazine article presented the foundation with an opportunity it could not afford to miss. With a vast new audience now aware of Canavan disease and its horrors, the foundation now had an opportunity to inform a broader audience than it ever had before of the fact that with carrier screening the disease could be prevented. With this in mind, the board voted to commit its resources to a major informational campaign to achieve this goal. Soon afterward, a national television program highlighted Canavan's disease. The foundation, aware of the previous situation, worked to contact local stations around the country that were carrying the program, asking them to insert a message on where further information on the disease was available. Several stations did indeed carry the message.

QUESTIONS TO ASK

1. If a major article or report about your organization or mission omits key information or is less than favorable, are you prepared to fill in the missing information or correct an error?

December 20, 1998

Dear Friends of the Canavan Foundation:

In "Keeping Jacob Alive" (Sunday, December 6, 1998), *The New York Times Magazine* ran a compelling story that captured the anguish and horror of Canavan disease. To the extent that the article heightened public awareness of this tragic illness, *The Times* is to be commended.

Yet while we at the Canavan Foundation were pleased that a publication as prestigious and widely read as *The New York Times* chose to focus its attention on a family's struggle with Canavan disease, we were equally dismayed by the lack of attention the article paid to information about the existence of reliable carrier screening and the ability at the present time to prevent the disease from occurring at all.

We felt it important to share with you our reaction to the article and the enclosed letter we sent to the Editor of the *Times Magazine* as our response. All of this has made our current program to inform and educate both the Jewish and the medical communities even more urgent.

We hope you will share this information with others who have seen and read the article in *The New York Times.*

Sincerely,

The Board of Directors

Letter from the Canavan Foundation board. Reprinted with permission.

2. Do you have a single spokesperson who, alone, will speak on behalf of your group?

LESSONS LEARNED

Never measure the significance of publicity solely on the basis of the size or the influence of the periodical in which it appears. Measure significance by the totality of the story. If it is less than complete, find aggressive ways to fill in the gaps.

LAST WORD

It's often not how much is written but what is *not* written that is important.

CHAPTER TWO

Making Your Event Special

SPECIAL EVENTS are part of the overall funding arsenal of many nonprofit institutions. Used wisely and carefully, they not only can bring in significant funds but also can provide a spotlight to focus on an organization's goals and areas of concern. In addition, they can be an effective tool to draw newcomers to an organization, to promote a specific mission or cause, or to draw volunteers into a new kind of organizational involvement.

Special events are no panacea, however, for an ailing funding program. A single event, except in rare circumstances, seldom serves as the only funding weapon used by an organization. Regardless of their primary purpose—whether for funding, for promotion, or for bringing supporters together—events that are planned haphazardly, without an awareness of physical, financial, seasonal, and personnel needs and without meticulous step-by-step planning, can cut deeply into an organization's work agenda. This results in a loss of time and a diversion of personnel from necessary activities. In some instances, these events can be financial fiascoes.

The special events discussed in this chapter range widely in scope and substance, from yearly events that have found a strong annual niche in the organization program to single events and series designed to meet a specific current need. They include an event that arguably may be the best-known and most successful of its kind and an event that was crafted quickly but carefully to meet an immediate need and was later revitalized to become an ongoing program. The cast of characters in these special events, like the agendas of the organizations, is varied and includes not only celebrities but also social secretaries and even college students.

In the best circumstances, as some of these cases demonstrate, an event not only can raise considerable sums of money but also can draw supporters into a deeper understanding of critical areas of concern and ideally into a stronger and more meaningful relationship with the organization.

The Big Picture

Capitalizing on Celebrity Involvement

BACKGROUND

In 1950, a group of parents whose children were afflicted by muscle disease founded the Muscular Dystrophy Association (MDA). A year later, it found an incredible resource. On December 28, 1951, Jerry Lewis, who costarred with Dean Martin on an NBC network television show, made his first national appeal for the MDA. That was the beginning of a relationship that drew Lewis closer into the MDA orbit as *volunteer extraordinaire,* who promoted the needs of the association and raised funds through other national broadcasts in the ensuing years.

○ CHALLENGE

As the organization grew from five affiliated chapters in 1951 to become a national organization with well over a hundred chapters dealing with over forty muscle disorders, its need for increased funding for research, for medical care, and for a wide range of nationwide services grew dramatically. It recognized the urgency of finding some way to reach out and attract a much broader audience than it had been reaching.

◑ PLAN

Lewis was now serving as national chairman, and the world-renowned entertainer was increasingly being recognized as the MDA's banner carrier. A decision was reached to capitalize on his popularity and his identification with the MDA. As most of the association's programs were funded by individual contributions, it was decided to take the MDA case directly to the public. In 1966, after garnering donated air time and with Lewis personally recruiting top figures in the entertainment field to appear, the first national Muscular Dystrophy Association Labor Day Telethon was aired.

● RESULT

The 1966 telethon not only raised over $1 million but also brought the message of the Muscular Dystrophy Association, and its challenges and needs, to millions of viewers, many hearing the message for the first time. From that beginning, the telethon has become a much anticipated annual event, setting new standards in dollars raised and viewership numbers earned along the way. Over the years, the telethon has raised close to $1 billion, including a record $53.1 million in 1999, when it was seen live by some seventy-five million viewers and when it became the world's first live multilingual Webcast. More than setting records, however, the telethon's success, along with the visibility it has given to the MDA program and achievements, has drawn new supporters to the cause, including a host of national and local sponsors. In addition, it has triggered local and national fundraising campaigns. Boosted by the telethon's success, the Muscular Dystrophy Association has vastly expanded its services and training as it has grown to an organization with 155 chapters and over two million

Flier for Muscular Dystrophy Association Worldwide Telethon.
Photo courtesy of MDA. Reprinted with permission.

volunteers, a summer camp program in over forty states, and a nationwide network of over 230 hospital-affiliated clinics. Befitting its achievements, the MDA and Jerry Lewis were presented with the American Medical Association's Lifetime Achievement Award "for significant and lasting contributions to the health and welfare of humanity." The MDA's award was the first ever given to a nonprofit organization.

QUESTIONS TO ASK

1. Have you looked to see if there is some charismatic figure who is interested in your cause and who might be willing to lend his or her personal involvement to the kind of event most suited to that figure?

2. Have you found ways to use a successful event as a launching pad for other, less ambitious events?

LESSONS LEARNED

If your organization is fortunate enough to attract a figure of national stature to identify with your cause, make sure that you find the vehicle best suited for making use of that individual's talents.

LAST WORD

Even a star can be a team player.

Shall We Dance?

Involving College Students as Fundraisers

BACKGROUND

In 1972, a fourteen-year-old Pennsylvania boy, Christopher Millard, who was dying from cancer, wrote an imaginative story, which he titled "The Four Diamonds," about a knight armed with four attributes—the diamonds of courage, wisdom, honesty, and strength—who battled an evil sorceress. He died soon afterward, and his parents, Charles and Irma Millard, recognizing both the emotional and financial difficulties they had experienced, decided to establish a fund in Christopher's memory to help ease the financial burdens of other families of children with cancer.

○ CHALLENGE

In 1973, after the Four Diamonds Fund was established at the nearby Milton S. Hershey Medical Center of Pennsylvania State University, the Millards took on the initial burden of acquiring support for the fund. Envisioning the development of a grassroots fundraising campaign in Pennsylvania communities, they began their campaign with a benefit concert of Brahms's *Requiem*, followed by such community events as garage and bake sales, charity volley-ball games, and flea markets throughout central Pennsyl-vania. Even though money was being raised and awareness of the fund's needs was reaching a wider audience, the Mil-lards recognized that they were struggling and that they needed a large breakthrough event with major funding po-tential if the campaign was to be a success.

◑ PLAN

In 1977, an event materialized. Pennsylvania State's Inter-fraternity Council, seeking to involve fraternity and soror-ity students in a funding event that could raise money for a local charity, agreed to sponsor a thirty-hour dance marathon to benefit the Four Diamonds Fund. The con-cept was simple. Prior to the February event, students would solicit pledges from students, townspeople, and compa-nies in support of participating dancers. Funding would be bolstered by competition among Greek organizations to see which fraternity or sorority could raise the most money. Recognizing the event's potential, fund leaders sup-ported the effort.

● RESULT

In its first year, the event drew thirty-nine couples and was much more successful as a fundraiser than any of the fund's previous events. That was only the beginning, however. With encouragement from the Four Diamonds Fund, the dance marathon became an annual event, with interest, participation, and funding increasing each year. Over its first five years, Thon, as it has come to be known, raised over $250,000, which resulted in 411 monetary allocations to 317 families. And then Thon really took off, both in participation and fundraising success. A forty-eight-hour event for many years, Thon now attracts over five hundred dancers and eighteen hundred volunteer planners. More than fifteen thousand student fundraisers solicit donations between November and February, and fraternities and sororities vie for the honor of raising the most money. In the process, Thon has become the nation's largest student-run philanthropy, having raised over $13 million for the fund, including a record $2.53 million in 1999, with two Greek letter societies each raising over $250,000. Its success also has been a boon to nonprofit causes elsewhere, as over forty schools throughout the country have launched dance marathons patterned after Thon to benefit their local charities. Its significance to the Four Diamond Fund is immeasurable, as funding from Thon accounts for some 82 percent of all its donations. Thon's importance became even more apparent in 1999 when its success gave impetus to a major new undertaking. Between 1999 and 2003, $1 million raised from each Thon, or $5 million overall, is being used to endow a new institute for pediatric cancer research at Pennsylvania State University's College of Medicine at the Milton S. Hershey Medical Center.

QUESTIONS TO ASK

1. Have you tapped every potential audience who might be interested in helping you raise funds?

2. Are you willing to let others operate a funding event in your behalf?

3. Have you provided detailed information on your cause, its importance, and how the funds that are raised will be used to those who are planning an event in your behalf?

LESSONS LEARNED

Never underestimate the ability of young people to get excited about a cause. If they do get excited about your cause and can have fun participating in it, they'll be among your most enthusiastic and successful volunteers.

LAST WORD

Youth isn't wasted on the young if you don't waste what the young can do for you.

The Pig That Saved the Y

Finding Funding Events to Meet an Immediate Need

BACKGROUND

Located between Buffalo and Niagara Falls in upstate New York, YWCA of the Tonawandas has served the blue-collar communities of Tonawanda and North Tonawanda since its founding in 1913 with a diverse program of sports and cultural activities aimed at a spectrum of participants ranging from preschoolers to seniors. Housed in two older buildings joined together, with a gymnasium added in the back, the Y, along with other institutions in the area, was in the economic doldrums in the mid-1990s.

○ CHALLENGE

YWCA of the Tonawandas was in danger of closing. It was a small operation with an overall budget of $220,000, and its accumulated deficit had reached $22,000 by November 1995. There was no income due for at least another month, and volunteers were running the organization.

◑ PLAN

Because of the immediate concern that there was not enough cash to keep the agency going, a quick funding event that could be developed and sold virtually overnight seemed to be an appropriate stopgap measure. The Y turned to an independent film broker, who served on the agency's board, to help find a second-run family movie that might be donated for a benefit showing. The broker not only was able to find an appropriate film, *Babe*, an animated feature about a pig, but also was helpful in putting the Y together with another group on whose board she served, the community's nonprofit Riviera Theater. The Riviera, which during the prior year had purchased its theater from the city through payment of back taxes, also was in need of a fundraising vehicle and an image-boosting activity. Within days, the groups reached an agreement on division of income, with the Y taking box office receipts and the Riviera keeping the income from refreshment stand sales. Before a week was out, two matinee showings were scheduled, promoted by press announcements and word of mouth.

● RESULT

The results were both immediate and long-term. The initial film showings, at an affordable 50 cents a head, drew lines of families to the eleven hundred–seat theater, and both showings were sellouts. These showings raised enough money to help the organization survive. In addition, the Y's involvement served as a tool to market its image and programs. Within months, a new director, Lynn Shaftic-Averill, was hired. Looking at the results of the film showings, she planned several more with the same concept.

The results again were sold-out performances. During the summer of 1996, discussions with the Riviera led to a decision to enlarge the concept and make the film showings an expanded, ongoing program. Since 1996, the Children's Film Festival Series, featuring G-rated and PG-rated films that have just finished their first runs but have not begun second runs, has become an annual community fixture. Generally running twice a day, at 11 A.M. and 1 P.M., for fifteen Saturdays from September through May, the series sells out most performances. Ticket prices have increased to a higher but still bargain price of $1, with the same financial arrangement between the two partner organizations in force. They also share advertising and promotional costs equally. As the event has increased in scope, it has drawn growing audiences, and its benefits to the Y have grown as well. The board member–film broker has been able to obtain original film posters, which are raffled off to benefit the Y at each showing, and audiences now bring in cans of food for its food pantry program. In 1998–1999, the Y netted $11,451 while promoting its programs through the film festival. "While the money is important," says Shaftic-Averill, "our single most important benefit has been to reestablish our name in the community as a leader in family programming. There isn't a family with kids in school that isn't aware that the YWCA is up and running."

QUESTIONS TO ASK

1. Have you tapped all the immediate resources available to you, including your board?

2. If a single event is successful, have you explored ways to expand it?

3. In a cooperative program, does your partner have as much to gain as you do?

LESSONS LEARNED

Faced with an urgent funding need, you should think of easily accessible ways to meet that need rather than focusing on more complex solutions. The people closest to you may help provide possible approaches. If a stopgap measure works, that's great; but perhaps that stopgap will have a longer life down the road, and perhaps a temporary success will become an ongoing success.

LAST WORD

If they like the movie, maybe they'll read the book—and you're the book.

Seeing Is Believing

Choosing Event Sites

BACKGROUND

Orbis has an unusual signature—a DC-10 aircraft. Using the world's only "flying eye hospital," Orbis sends volunteer doctors and its plane, converted to serve as an eye surgery hospital and classroom, to developing countries. The volunteers teach local ophthalmologists, nurses, and other health care workers how to treat the causes of blindness while treating the patients as well. Since its founding in 1982, Orbis has conducted hundreds of programs in seventy-nine countries and has trained forty-two thousand workers to provide treatment and training in their own countries.

○ CHALLENGE

Aware that most people are extremely impressed any time they actually see the Orbis plane and witness how and where the volunteer doctors do their work, organization leaders knew that if they could bring the plane to a place where supporters and potential donors could actually see it, it would give a major boost to Orbis's fundraising efforts. Although for 80 percent of the year, the plane is nowhere near the Orbis headquarters in New York City, an opportunity presented itself early in 1999 for Orbis to bring the plane to the New York area. This provided Orbis with the opening it needed to plan a first-time funding event built around the airplane.

◑ PLAN

Although the plane could be flown to John F. Kennedy Airport (JFK) in Queens, New York, there were several issues that had to be addressed—where to house the plane at the airport so that people could board it, how to plan a major funding event with broad appeal, and how to lessen any possible resistance from potential attendees to traveling to and from JFK, one of the world's busiest airports, which is some distance from midtown Manhattan. In response to the first concern, Orbis leaders called on executives of the Port Authority of New York and New Jersey to see if they might be able to offer a site at JFK where the DC-10 could be housed and the event could be held. Fortunately, Port Authority officials responded to the Orbis request and found a giant space, Hangar 19, usually used for maintenance. Although the hangar had been used for community-related events in the past, it had never before been used for a fundraising event; however, because Orbis had to have a large indoor venue at an airport and because the Port Authority was eager to support a significant aviation-related charity, it made an exception and charged only a modest fee. To increase the appeal of an airport event, Orbis turned to a longtime supporter, United Airlines. United's maintenance crews have provided many free hours of maintenance service and have donated parts to the Orbis plane. In addition, the airline has flown volunteer doctors to where the DC-10 is located and has trained many Orbis pilots, and many United pilots have flown the

Orbis plane as volunteers. United also had a maintenance facility on the other side of the hangar from where the reception was to be held. Even more serendipitous was the fact that the chairman of United Airlines, Gerald Greenwald, would be retiring in the near future. Because Greenwald had many friends in the airline industry, the event also could be a surprise retirement party for him. The concern that attendees might not relish the thought of attending an event at an airport turned out to be minor, although planners did offer bus transportation to and from JFK as part of the ticket cost.

● RESULT

Considering the scope of the undertaking, the lead time was quite short. With an April 1999 date set, planning commenced in December 1998. Despite the two-pronged appeal of the event—the honoring of Greenwald and the private tours of the DC-10 to be made available throughout the evening—a special theme was added to the mix. As the DC-10 would be going to Morocco after its U.S. stay, they dubbed the party, A Moroccan Fantasy. The invitation cover showed an airplane flying through the silhouette of a Moroccan arch. The mailing list, aimed at Orbis supporters as well as airline industry officials and friends and associates of Greenwald, consisted of twenty-five hundred, with a hoped-for return of 400. Tables of ten were sold for $25,000, $10,000, and $5,000; individual tickets were sold for $1,000 and $500, with donors offered cocktails, dinner, dancing, and a tour of the DC-10. Although the mailing didn't go out until some four weeks prior to the event, it drew a more-than-expected turnout of 425 and netted about $300,000. As important as the funding was, the exposure to Orbis and its program was equally significant. Having supporters learn about the Orbis mission by actually boarding the flying hospital reaped giant benefits for the organization. For many attendees, it marked the beginning of an emotional tie to Orbis and its work. According to Melanie Brandston, Orbis's director of major gifts, "Our message came across quite dramatically. A huge majority of our guests knew little about Orbis in advance, but I learned that on a scale of one to ten, people rated the event an eleven. In fact, many people, learning about the Orbis mission for the first time, have been eager to help us in any way that they can."

QUESTIONS TO ASK

1. Have you presented your case as dramatically as you can?

2. Have you called on all the resources available to you to plan a special event?

3. Even after having found several elements crucial to a special event, have you asked if there are any other elements you might add to enhance its appeal?

CPR for Nonprofits

Invitation for Orbis fundraiser, A Moroccan Fantasy. Graphic design by H-Design for Orbis International, New York, NY. Reprinted with permission.

LESSONS LEARNED

If you have a story to tell and an audience to tell it to, the visual impact of an event site that dramatizes your story can be your most powerful weapon.

LAST WORD

Choosing the right site can be insightful—and important.

Hitting the Target

Refocusing Events
to Promote Priorities

BACKGROUND

Since its founding in 1920, the American Cancer Society, and its local divisions throughout the country, have played a leading role in public education and in the funding of needed research on cancer. A key force in its activities over the years has been its five divisions in New York and one in New Jersey, which in 1998 were linked together as the American Cancer Society, Eastern Division. Although the national society has supported research on all forms of cancer, it saw a need in the nineties to focus on a specific cancer issue of growing concern—the prevalence of breast cancer.

○ CHALLENGE

Aware of the need to specifically target breast cancer, the six divisions that now constitute the eastern division decided to restructure their marketing and public relations approach to achieve that objective.

◑ PLAN

The new approach that was developed was designed to lead up to a specific event that had been successful in the past but that was renamed to emphasize its new focus. Thus the five-mile annual cancer walk, Making Strides Against Cancer, was officially renamed Making Strides Against Breast Cancer and was introduced in 1995. It has been held annually since then and since 1998 in New York City under the sponsorship of the eastern division. Although there are other cancer walks, this one, held the third Sunday in October, is the last walk of the year. A key to the new approach was its goal of finding ways to involve participants not only in the actual event but also in preparations leading up to it. The overall plan begins to take shape in January, following several months of initial planning, which begins immediately after the preceding walk has ended. It is in January that specific details and assignment of responsibilities are outlined. By March, staff and volunteers are assigned to a specific responsibility with a specific goal. One of the key goals is for participants to recruit one or more qualified potential captains—each of whom will eventually head a team of twenty-five—to attend the event's kickoff breakfast in August. To find qualified potential captains prior to the breakfast, the "stride recruitment team" (consisting of up to a hundred participants) divides up names found in corporate directories of New York companies and calls hundreds of these companies to find employees who are interested in women's issues or in breast cancer specifically. Interestingly, those who are recruited are asked only to attend the breakfast and are not recruited for the walk itself. While callers are concentrating solely on getting people to the breakfast, other staff and volunteers take on additional assignments, such as publicity, logistics, day-of-activities preparation, and printed materials. At the breakfast, which draws about nine hundred people and is designed to last only one hour, attendees learn more about the walk's goal and the ongoing fight against breast cancer. Those individuals potentially qualified as captains leave with shopping bags jammed with materials to help them recruit team participants, whose job it will be to attract others to participate in the walk. They also receive walk sweatshirts. The captains hang posters in their corporate facilities. These are reinforced by subway posters, radio and television spots, and other ads and publicity. After the breakfast, staff and volunteers adhere to a specific timetable, which indicates precisely what will happen on the days leading up to the event itself. Included in the timetable is a series of eight scripted messages, which, beginning in late August, captains are asked to send by e-mail or voice message to their coworkers.

● RESULT

Since the new marketing concept was introduced, the event has taken off incredibly. In 1998, for example, 14,000 people participated in the walk, which grossed $1.4 million. A portion of all money raised by the eastern division and sixteen other divisions around the country went to the society's national breast cancer research program. The following year, 1999, was even better; the walk attracted 20,500 walkers and grossed an estimated $1.85 million. In addition to its fundraising benefits, the walk, with its specific focus, continues to raise awareness among women on caring for themselves and having mammograms as needed. Also, by focusing on breast cancer, the walk clearly demonstrates that the American Cancer Society considers breast cancer an issue of tremendous concern.

QUESTIONS TO ASK

1. If you have a key issue on which to focus, have you directed your marketing effort to that specific issue?

2. Have you developed a plan that both motivates and involves your volunteers?

3. Have you tried to find new and creative tactics and ways to broaden your circle of supporters?

LESSONS LEARNED

When you're planning an event of major proportions, you may benefit considerably in the long run if you develop a detailed program designed to involve participants in the planning process as well as in the actual event.

LAST WORD

Good vision means a clear focus.

Site Specific

Raising Consciousness While Raising Funds

BACKGROUND

The Nature Conservancy was founded in 1951 with a specific focus—to save the world's ecosystems. The international organization, which has protected millions of acres of land since its founding and has become the largest private conservation effort in the world, has an office in every state. Over the years, it has attracted nearly a million members. Its Last Great Places Program: An Alliance for People and the Environment, which calls attention to endangered areas that should be saved, surpassed its five-year goal in 1995, raising $315 million.

○ CHALLENGE

The New York office of the conservancy did an excellent job of projecting the goals and challenges of the conservancy, but it maintained a fairly low profile and lacked the physical presence common to museums and performing arts groups. Fearful of complacency on the part of its supporters, the office was seeking a dramatic site-oriented special event to emphasize the urgency of its program.

◐ PLAN

Reviewing a wide range of options, national board member Carter F. Bales and then New York office head, Rona Shuman Kiley, concluded that an event relating to the major conservancy program, the Last Great Places, could capture widespread attention, raise a substantial amount of money, and dramatically focus on the organizational mission. Moreover, New York City's Central Park offered them a perfect venue for an event that could be presented in association with a logical partner, the Central Park Conservancy.

● RESULT

The First Great Party to Save the Last Great Places was presented in 1994, and it clearly and dramatically reflected the urgency of the conservancy mission. Some fifteen hundred guests attended a "blue jeans and black tie" party. They "traveled" to five of the world's most significant ecosystems, each re-created in specially constructed "ecotents," which through setting, wildlife, food, and entertainment evoked the splendor of a particular endangered area. This first party—it has been repeated every two years—also established several program aspects that have been maintained at each succeeding party, including a "Big Fish" award for notable preservation activity by an individual, an auction of one major "ecotour," and the singing of "Home on the Range" by a star-studded chorus of conservancy supporters. Each of the events has been widely publicized, has won many new supporters to the cause, and—not incidentally—has netted over $1 million.

Invitation to Nature Conservancy event. Designed by Pat Scully
Design. Reprinted with permission.

QUESTIONS TO ASK

1. Is your mission as clear to your constituents and supporters as it is to you?

2. If your special events do not articulate your mission, what steps can you take to refocus these events, without diminishing your funding potential?

LESSONS LEARNED

An event does not have to be grandiose to achieve both financial and motivational goals. It has to be on target. Dramatic impact can be a powerful tool to help you get your message across to your supporters. If you want maximum results, make sure that the medium you use has authenticity and visual appeal.

LAST WORD

Your message is your medium. Use every opportunity you have to promote your mission to your audiences.

An Eventful Campaign

Using Special Events to Provide Visibility

BACKGROUND

The Greenwich Public Library, in Greenwich, Connecticut, began its existence as a reading room before the turn of the nineteenth century and saw its first permanent library building erected in 1895. Moving to its current location in the upwardly mobile Connecticut community in 1960, the library has since experienced widespread involvement from townspeople, with usage increasing by around 3 percent a year. About 90 percent of local residents currently hold library cards.

○ CHALLENGE

As the library increased its services, it faced an urgent need to modernize and expand both its main facility and its branch in nearby Cos Cob to serve its growing number of users. With insufficient income in the town budget to finance the improvements, the library had to win approval from the town's planning board for a fund drive. In 1996, having received the go-ahead, the library launched a $10 million capital campaign. Although the library's need was real, there was some concern among its leaders that few people would take the drive seriously because the library had recently received a $25 million bequest from the estate of Clementine Lockwood Peterson to honor both her late husband, a prominent businessman, and her son, a musician who had passed away at an early age. The gift, which was designated for the library's business and music services, was not intended to replace public funding but was given instead to enhance those two specific areas of library operation.

◑ PLAN

The initial campaign budget did not include specific goals for different aspects of the drive. But Harrison Edwards, a consulting firm brought in to advise library leaders, suggested that a program of special events, bolstered by direct mail, could play a key role in providing public visibility to the drive and could raise as much as $350,000. This figure was later adopted as the goal for special community events. On the recommendation of its consultants, the library moved ahead with a two-year agenda of events, designed for different levels of affordability and interest, including a kickoff parade from one end of town to the other. The parade emphasized the library's service for more than a hundred years by featuring classic automobiles, which highlighted its Drive for the Drive theme. An automobile from every era was represented. Other public events planned included a family fair, a community open house, a concert and auction, the obligatory black tie gala, and a number of programs involving local personalities. Actress Glenn Close, who grew up in Greenwich and was one of three honorary campaign chairs, arranged for her film *101 Dalmatians* to be previewed in Greenwich. Resident Kathie Lee Gifford hosted a holiday program, and author John Jakes, a Greenwich resident, moderated a literary symposium featuring William F. Buckley, Bette Bao Lord, and Sandra Brown. A business awards dinner, a fundraiser, honored a local resident known for his international corporate leadership. The overall program attracted so much attention that Baccarat contacted the library to arrange a benefit party to celebrate the opening of its new store in town. The attention focused on the campaign by the events was heightened by a campaign brochure, a campaign newsletter sent as local newspaper supplements to the entire community, and a final direct-mail fund appeal. To add a sense of fun and visual interest, a fictitious library mascot, Dewey D. Digger, Bookworm, was created. His image appeared in ads, posters, signage, and a coloring book used as an invitation for a children's event.

● RESULT

The overall drive, which garnered tremendous press coverage, was a huge success, raising $11,250,000 and exceeding the campaign goal by over 10 percent. The special events and direct mail alone, boosted by the corporate dinner, which netted $450,000, nearly tripled its goal by raising $1 million. As an added boost, the visibility given to the library has since helped focus increased interest and support for its programs.

QUESTIONS TO ASK

1. If ardor in your fund drive is lacking at its onset, have you looked at developing special events that will kindle interest?

2. Have you found ways to focus on the entire community rather than only on specific funding targets?

3. Have you used a key community resource, its best-known people?

LESSONS LEARNED

If you want to win support from every stratum of the community, it will be useful to find ways to reach each of those publics, not only with mailings and advertising but also with events and activities that relate your program to your audiences.

LAST WORD

It isn't just who you know that's important, but who knows you.

When Ladies Lunch

Choosing Social Events That Reflect Organizational Identity

BACKGROUND

The Woodrow Wilson House in Washington, D.C., a National Trust historic site, was the residence of the former president of the United States, who lived there from 1921, after his term in office ended, until his death in 1924. Given to the National Trust in 1954, the house remained occupied by the president's widow, Edith Wilson, until she passed away in 1961. Two years later, with a mission to focus on the Wilson presidency and Wilson's legacy as educator, statesman, and world leader, the Woodrow Wilson House was opened to the public.

○ CHALLENGE

The Wilson House was looking for a special event in 1999 that not only would attract a high-profile audience and promote its programs but also would advance its mission, to focus on the Wilson presidency and areas related to it. Discussing these needs with the board, one trustee, Letitia Baldrige, social secretary to Jacqueline Kennedy, came up with an intriguing possibility—to have Wilson House host a first-ever reunion of former White House social secretaries.

◑ PLAN

The key to the event, as the Wilson staff recognized immediately, was its ability to attract as large a number of former White House social secretaries as possible. With Baldrige agreeing to serve as cochair, the pieces fell into place. Ann Stock, a former Clinton social secretary working at the Kennedy Center, was asked and accepted a role as cochair; and Capricia Marshall, the Clinton White House social secretary, agreed to serve as honorary chair. In addition, popular local television anchor Kathleen Matthews agreed to moderate a panel discussion among the former social secretaries. With its leadership set, the Wilson staff called all former social secretaries going back to the Truman administration and received enthusiastic responses, with sixteen social secretaries, all but two of those contacted, agreeing to come and all paying their own way to do so. With room for 150 attendees seated under a tent on the Wilson House garden lawn, the question of how much to charge became the biggest planning hurdle. Finally, after a great deal of discussion, the feeling prevailed that the luncheon should be a relatively affordable attraction, at $125 a person, rather than a "big bucks" $500-a-plate fundraiser.

● RESULT

Held on a weekday in June, Lunch with the White House Social Secretaries, featuring behind-the-scenes stories by each of the secretaries about their years in the White

House, captured the public imagination. With board members preselling tables of ten by telephone and letters, the event was a sellout. It also was a promotional bonanza for the Wilson House, with C-SPAN taping the event and exceptionally good press coverage. The reaction was so favorable that the Woodrow Wilson House considered developing such follow-up events—all focusing on aspects of the presidency—as luncheons featuring presidential press secretaries or State Department protocol chiefs.

QUESTIONS TO ASK

1. Have you determined the specific goal you wish to achieve from an event you sponsor?

2. If the event is closely related to your mission, do you have access to people closely related to that mission who can help make it a success?

3. If an event is successful, do you have a structure in place that allows you to undertake follow-up events?

LESSONS LEARNED

Special events need not always be designed as major fund-raisers. If they further the organization's mission and can be developed with volunteer help and support, they are worth undertaking.

LAST WORD

When you're mission driven, the ride is a smooth one.

The Main Event

Planning Innovative Affairs

BACKGROUND

Southampton College of Long Island University is located in one of America's most glittering summer playgrounds, the Hamptons beach area of New York. Founded in 1963 as the university's third branch, the college serves about twenty-five hundred students, most of whom are from other areas, with programs in marine biology and professional writing among its major academic draws.

○ CHALLENGE

Many of the area's fundraising events are successful because they attract the glitterati who can afford to pay top dollar for food, decor, and setting. Knowing it couldn't compete with that type of fundraiser, Southampton College was looking for an event that could net more than the $50,000 raised at one of its usual programs, typically a Hampton-type gala or cocktail party. When Rusty Leaver, a neighbor in nearby Montauk and owner of the Deep Hollow Ranch, broke the traditional Hampton funding mode, the college saw its opportunity. Leaver had hosted a benefit, the Back at the Ranch rock concert, in 1990. Instead of attracting the few at a high fee, the concert attracted many more paying much less, and it raised $270,000 for the imperiled Montauk Lighthouse fund. "We not only wanted to raise money but we wanted to expose our campus to a broad range of people who didn't know too much about us," said Timothy Bishop, the college provost. "We thought if we could adapt the Leaver concept and do a rock concert our own way for a large audience, we could achieve our goals."

◑ PLAN

In the summer of 1992, the college received a permit for fifty-five hundred people to attend its first rock concert, featuring Crosby, Stills, and Nash. Thanks to a professional contact, the college was able to enter into a promotional partnership with New York radio station WNEW, which featured free spots promoting the concert.

● RESULT

The first event netted a respectable $60,000 for the college's scholarship fund and attracted many first-time visitors to the college campus. Building on that beginning and with major support from the school's administration (Chancellor Robert F. X. Sillerman and his wife, Laura, have chaired the event in recent years), the concert has grown into an annual event. In a cooperative spirit, concert dates are now cleared in advance with the Leaver concert to avoid possible conflicts. Thanks to a stronger emphasis on selling reserved tables in recent years, at $6,000 to $50,000 a table, the concert has brought in increasing amounts of money and has considerably raised the visibility of the college, which has seen its enrollment grow over the years. In 1999, the event, which sells general admission tickets at $40 and VIP seating at $300, drew a sellout crowd of seventy-five hundred and raised $1.1 million for the college's scholarship fund.

QUESTIONS TO ASK

1. Have you clearly defined what results, other than money, you might wish to achieve?

2. Have you explored all options, including looking at what other groups have tried, before deciding on what you will do?

3. If you are modeling your program on another event, have you made sure that you have differentiated your approach to meet your own specific needs?

LESSONS LEARNED

Even if it is similar on the surface to other events, each special event should have its own signature. Make sure that yours does.

LAST WORD

Adapt, don't adopt.

Making Your Event Special

CHAPTER THREE

Asking
for
Money

I DON'T USUALLY pay too much attention to bumper stickers. One I saw several years ago, however, has remained firmly in my mind for the directness of its message. It read simply, "Fundraisers are asking for it."

Asking, as any development director obviously knows, goes with the territory; but as most development directors also know, it isn't always that simple. Some key questions must be addressed first, such as who does the asking, who is asked, when are they asked, why are they asked, how are they asked, and for what are they asked?

Fundraising, as the cases in this chapter illustrate, is far from a routine endeavor. Even the most ardent organizational benefactors may have other pressing issues that compete for their support. Although careful research, urgency of need, the potency of the case, and the vitality of leadership are all key elements of a successful funding program, perhaps the most vital component in the funder's arsenal is sensitivity to the donor and the donor's needs. (Such is the kind of sensitivity I feel I exercised in resisting my original temptation to title this chapter "How to Harry a Millionaire.") Listening, waiting, and sharing are all key aspects of the total effort. Undue pressure isn't. The ability to listen and then react is an important element in several of these cases, as is the ability to engender involvement, not only with the prospective donor but also with those within the organization. It is worth remembering that whether you are moving to a new funding level or making a new funding start, the ultimate success of any campaign is based on successful relationships rather than on instant gratification.

You're the Top

Moving Major Donors Up to New Funding Heights

BACKGROUND

Iowa State University, one of the nation's oldest land-grant institutions, was chartered by the state as the Iowa Agricultural College and Model Farm in 1858 and opened its doors to its first class in 1868. Renamed the Iowa State College of Agriculture and Mechanic Arts in 1898, it took its official present name, the Iowa State University of Science and Technology, in 1959. Although its agricultural heritage has led it into pioneering activities in that field, it has since become a broad-based institution with recognized programs in such other areas as materials science, engineering, physical science, and family and consumer science.

○ CHALLENGE

Iowa State University had been the recipient of major gifts over the years, but until 1993, no gift had exceeded $3 million. When Martin C. Gischke was named university president in 1991, he laid out what he termed "a bold new vision," with a stated goal to make Iowa State "the best land grant university in the nation." As he indicated, however, this lofty objective could be achieved only if there was a major infusion of funds. New support would be needed to significantly increase student scholarships, to complete several important capital projects, and to strengthen academic centers of excellence, including the university's College of Agriculture, a key entity in any land-grant university's educational program. He suggested to the Iowa State University Foundation, the university's fundraising arm, that major gifts by individuals had to increase to a new and vastly higher level in order to realize the ambitious program he envisioned.

◑ PLAN

The foundation responded to the president's challenge by intensifying its efforts to identify and cultivate those current donors who might share Gischke's vision. The president, meanwhile, made himself available to the foundation, indicating that he personally would meet and discuss the university's future path with any potential individual donors who demonstrated strong interest in moving to a much higher level of support. Although the effort was all encompassing, the strategy moved forward at a careful and deliberate pace to ensure that potential donors would feel little pressure and would have sufficient time to consider their positions. When Thomas J. Mitchell took over as foundation president in 1997, the partnership between the university president and the foundation moved to an even more intensive level. The plan included the foundation's strengthening its relationship with current donors and identifying new individuals that would have interest in this bold initiative.

● RESULT

In the space of several years, Gischke, at times accompanied by key administration and faculty members, visited those individuals identified as having the interest and capability to support his vision at a higher level. By spring 1997, the results of the drive began to come into clear focus. One couple, who had been large donors over the years, made a major move upward with a pledge of $7 million. The next year, the university won pledges of $9 million and $10 million from two other couples, and a $15 million pledge from a donor who wished to remain anonymous. The benefits of longtime cultivation and the personal involvement of the president became even more evident. A local couple who had been supporters of the university since the sixties and had contributed gifts of up to $4 million told the president that they would be making a significant bequest to the university. The couple had been meeting with the president from time to time since 1992, when, at a luncheon, he had first laid out the details of his ambitious goal of developing a world-class department of agronomy. The size of the couple's bequest was not known until 1999, when, after both members of the couple had passed away, the terms of the will were revealed. The couple, who requested anonymity, gave an $80 million gift to the university, designated specifically for the Department of Agronomy. It was the largest individual donation ever made to the university.

QUESTIONS TO ASK

1. If your organization plans to move to a new level of funding, do you have a bold and exciting vision to share with potential donors?

2. Have you identified a passionate and articulate spokesperson who will give the time and energy needed to convey your message, and do you have a professional development team to facilitate the process?

3. Have you clearly and carefully identified those few special individuals who care enough about your overall cause that you sense they would be moved to increase their giving dramatically to achieve a major new goal?

4. Can you use the major gifts you've already received to leverage even higher gifts from others?

LESSONS LEARNED

Personal, yet unpressured, cultivation of major donors over a period of time does not slow down your funding effort. On the contrary, in the long run, it will help raise your donors to an even higher level of giving.

LAST WORD

An $80 million gift isn't chicken feed, but it sure can nourish an agronomy program.

Pitching for a Cause

Letting Celebrities Determine Their Involvement in Fund Drives

BACKGROUND

The Westchester Medical Center in Valhalla, New York, began as a United States Army hospital during World War I, when it was used to treat victims of the Spanish influenza epidemic. In 1920, after the Army had turned the facility over to Westchester County, it began life anew as Grasslands Hospital, serving as a key area treatment center over the next half century for victims of such epidemics as polio and tuberculosis. Its transformation into a modern medical center began in the fifties and culminated in 1977 with its rebirth as the Westchester Medical Center, in a newly built regional medical facility. Several decades later, operating as an independent institution, the center decided to meet a long-felt need, to build a special facility for children. In 1997, the Children's Hospital Foundation was created to raise $25 million of the $145 million it would cost to build a new children's hospital. The additional funds were to come from the center's assumption of a long-term debt. Because the center was previously a county facility, it had never conducted a major fund drive.

It was clear that to meet this new challenge, the need for the new children's hospital had to be clearly and boldly articulated.

○ CHALLENGE

The parent of a former patient, a builder, who had been impressed with the medical expertise and compassion of hospital staff after his daughter had been misdiagnosed at another hospital, told clients, whose new home he was building, about the need for the new children's hospital. Those clients were New York Yankee baseball great, David Cone, and his wife, Lynn. Impressed with what they heard, the Cones decided that they wanted to help the hospital campaign. Development staff members of the Children's Hospital Foundation met with Lynn Cone, and instead of suggesting their own course of action, they brainstormed to find out what type of involvement with the campaign she and her husband might like.

◐ PLAN

With their new home nearing completion, the Cones agreed to host a housewarming party as a benefit for the new children's hospital. To add spark to the event, David Cone invited the Yankee team to attend and meet the donors. With about a third of the team attending, the $300 a person housewarming–wine tasting party drew some two hundred guests and helped articulate the need for the hospital. After the event, further discussions led to David Cone's donation of baseball memorabilia for a live auction. A year later, in 1997, the Cones came up with an idea that had strong promotional and funding potential. David would host a baseball clinic prior to a Yankee game for youngsters, who would have the opportunity to participate in coaching sessions and batting practice with the Yankees. David, who was able to convince the Yankee hierarchy to agree to the event, paid for all the food and drink and arranged for the children to receive autographed pictures of themselves with Yankee stars. Parents and sponsors paid $1,000 for each of the seventy-five youngsters who participated. The event was repeated in 1998 and 1999, when a number of disadvantaged youngsters were sponsored by a growing number of donors. Prior to that event, with many donors by then aware of the Cones' support of the hospital, David and Lynn had hosted a $500-a-person anniversary party to benefit the campaign.

● RESULT

The personal involvement of the Cones gave tremendous visibility to the fund drive. It also helped attract and cultivate a significant number of new donors who have since become actively involved in the effort. By summer 1999, the drive could directly attribute about a third of a million dollars raised to the Cone's involvement and even more indirectly. Both Cones also have contributed far beyond their fundraising participation. David, without fanfare, has made himself accessible to young patients, including meeting—in the middle of a busy season—with a patient with a severe disability at the center's request. Lynn has become an active trustee of the Children's Hospital Foundation.

QUESTIONS TO ASK

1. If a figure of note has become interested in your cause, have you tried to find out in what way that person wishes to be involved before imposing your views?

2. Do you take care in your promotional activities not to overuse your celebrity?

3. Have you developed a marketing plan to tie the celebrity to your program?

LESSONS LEARNED

Instead of "sparing" celebrities from details concerning their involvement in a campaign, try speaking to them first to see how they perceive their involvement. Brainstorming may not always work, but if it does, you may discover that some celebrities might be willing to contribute even more than you had anticipated.

LAST WORD

If donors can become emotionally involved in your cause, so can celebrities.

The Big Bang

Shifting Stalled Funding Efforts into Overdrive

BACKGROUND

Boston University, a private university with an endowment of under $100 million, had averaged, by 1981, only $4.9 million annually from fundraising over the prior fifteen years and had failed on three attempts during that period to launch major fundraising campaigns.

○ CHALLENGE

Analyzing the university's needs for the coming decade, leaders determined that half a billion dollars over and above its operating budget was required to meet the demands of its educational and research programs. Faced with this stark realization, however, the university knew that with the development program then in place, there was little chance of meeting its goal. Recognizing the urgency of reaching its objectives, President John R. Silber decided to take immediate steps to accelerate the funding program.

◐ PLAN

In 1981, Silber hired Robert Feldman, a top professional with major successes elsewhere, to reorganize the development program. Moving decisively and quickly, Feldman staffed and consolidated the development program into three areas—alumni relations, university relations, and development. This move, together with competent leadership and direction, helped increase annual giving from $4.9 million to $24.2 million in just three years. With a giving pattern established and a professional operation in place, the stage was set for the launching of a major capital campaign, a decision made following a feasibility study for a $200 million capital campaign undertaken by The Brakeley, John Price Jones, the firm later retained to provide full-time resident campaign direction. The drive, approved by the Boston University board in 1983, was organized so that each of the university's academic deans played a major leadership role, turning the campaign, in effect, into sixteen college (or school) campaigns run simultaneously.

● RESULT

Although there were challenges to be met in each stage of the campaign, the overall result was nothing short of astounding. The university reached its $200 million goal in its fifth year, boosted by a $19 million gift brought in by Silber, six pledges of $1 million or more by trustees during the campaign's quiet phase, and 100 percent giving by the executive staff, deans, and trustees. The first challenge confronting the campaign occurred during the first six months, when the designated campaign chairman became too ill to assume the role, and no replacement of his stature could be found. On the advice of its counsel, the university substituted an office of the chairman with a group of executive officers, who shared the responsibilities. This arrangement allowed for their utilization on selected tasks consistent with their expertise, time, and interest. Later, after the campaign had been announced, a shortage of volunteers threatened the success of the individual college-level phase, making it difficult to reach alumni. A series of orientation and training sessions for each of the deans overcame this difficulty by preparing the deans for stepped-up roles in the campaign. Despite the temporary setbacks, the drive accelerated each year. In its fifth year, it reached its goal with all-time record annual giving of $58.6 million. The drive provided such momentum, in fact, that on its completion Silber announced the launching of the $1 billion Turn of the Century Fund.

QUESTIONS TO ASK

1. Have you ensured total participation at all top levels in your drive?

2. When you recognize the need to recruit top professionals, do you follow through?

3. Do you view setbacks as temporary deterrents rather than defeats?

LESSONS LEARNED

Past funding failures do not necessarily doom an organization to future failures. A careful look at your prospects by top professionals and the development of an approach that draws on an organization's strength and personally involves its key constituency can turn a negative picture into a positive result.

LAST WORD

If you want professional results, take a professional approach.

A Joint Effort

Developing Cooperative Funding Events

BACKGROUND

Three small nonprofit organizations, linked together by their service to young people and by interlocking relationships among several of their board members, were having difficulty in finding the funds to meet the expanding needs of their programs.* One, a young organization for infants and children with cancer disorders founded in 1997, had little public name recognition but had a prestigious board. Although it had a worthy cause to plead, it had to compete with its own hospital's other services for grants. The second organization of longer standing, which had built its reputation as one of the nation's most respected arts-in-education programs in the country, had good name recognition and an excellent reputation for its theatrical productions focusing on substance abuse. As a grassroots organization, however, its board was dedicated to its cause and helpful in many areas but had little financial clout. The third nonprofit organization, which had been founded in 1973, had an outreach program

*The three organizations have asked not to be identified by name.

focused on protecting children from abuse and neglect while giving families the tools that would enable them to stay together in a happier and emotionally healthier environment. It had excellent name recognition in the local community that it served and a board of financially prominent individuals.

○ CHALLENGE

Each organization had tapped the funding sources for the areas it served to the full extent of its capabilities. All three organizations, separately, recognized that the way to get to a higher level of giving might be through a unique fundraising event with the potential of substantial returns. Yet even though their board members were generous in their support, most didn't have the time to become involved in planning a funding event to meet organizational needs.

◑ PLAN

Because of an interesting coincidence (that a financial executive not only happened to be president of both the cancer-concerned and arts-in-education organizations but also was a business partner of the man who was president of the third organization), a plan was put into motion to involve all three organizations in a unique partnership. Recognizing their common cause of serving children and knowing that each board had members with strong ties to the Wall Street community, the organizations decided to band together and pool their resources to present a single annual event, a dinner and celebrity auction to benefit all three organizations equally. With a generic name for the event, which both emphasized its purpose as a fundraiser for organizations providing strong support for children's causes and allowed for additions or changes in the beneficiary organizations if needed, the event has been held annually since 1997.

RESULT

With each organization's board contributing to the event and their finance-oriented members proving especially proficient in tapping their Wall Street compatriots to purchase tables for the dinner, the event has been a resounding success. With expenses kept to a bare minimum, the most recent dinner raised well over $200,000 for each organization.

QUESTIONS TO ASK

1. If you've shared materials or even venues with other organizations, might it be feasible to pool resources for an event?

2. Have you thoroughly analyzed what specific resources your organization can bring to a partnership and what other organizations can bring to you?

3. Are you willing to submerge your individual identity to find greater overall returns?

LESSONS LEARNED

Organizations that serve the same audience might find in that commonality a bridge to beneficial common activities.

LAST WORD

Cooperation can be a powerful tool for prying open donor pocketbooks.

The First Million

Responding to Challenging Opportunities

BACKGROUND

In 1986, Chicago actress Barbara Gaines founded a workshop in Shakespearean performance that became a showcase known as the Shakespeare Repertory Theater. In a matter of years, the fledgling operation grew to become the Chicago Shakespeare Theater (CST), a resident professional theater company recognized as a major force on the local arts scene. As the company's performance schedule increased, it launched other key programs, including Team Shakespeare, an innovative instruction program for Chicago's school system, which reached over thirty-five thousand students and eleven hundred teachers both at the theater and in the schools. The budget grew along with the program, from under $500,000 to over $3 million in twelve years.

○ CHALLENGE

By 1996, it was evident that the company's performing space, a cramped dance and recital hall that seated only 330, was no longer viable. Gaines, executive director Criss

Henderson, and the board began to explore all available space options—purchasing its performance space and refurbishing it, buying an existing theater and remodeling it, or building a completely new theater. All options seemed beyond the capabilities of a theater whose annual giving, 50 percent of its budget, still had not reached the $1 million mark and whose annual donors numbered under fifteen hundred. A feasibility study, which showed that the theater's maximum fundraising capability in a capital campaign would be only $6 million to $7 million, put a further damper on the idea of moving ahead with building plans. Just when the theater despaired of owning its own space, a totally unexpected fourth option presented itself. The head of Chicago's Metropolitan Pier and Exposition Authority approached the CST to ask if it would be interested in establishing a new theater on Navy Pier, the city's multimillion-dollar entertainment redevelopment project on Lake Michigan. The city would build the facility to the CST's specifications, and the theater's only obligation would be to pay the $4 million cost of building out the theater's interior and the cost of leasing back the space for ninety years. Although the offer was more than tempting, the theater's leaders agonized over the site, a hurly-burly entertainment and tourist center, and the $12 million needed not only for the facility but also for ongoing operations and a first-time endowment. They finally agreed that this was a once-in-a-lifetime opportunity that they couldn't afford to miss.

◑ PLAN

Planning for the campaign began in 1997, with the recognition that three leadership gifts of $1 million or more were needed as a launching pad for the company's first multimillion dollar campaign, this despite the fact that the theater's largest individual gift prior to that date had been $60,000. With the help of an outside funding agency, three prospects with a connection to either the theater or its founder were identified, and a scenario to approach each was carefully scripted. One was a current board member who had been involved in the Navy Pier negotiations and had given, soon afterward, an unsolicited gift of $500,000. A second candidate was an area businessman who sat on a university board with Gaines, the theater's founder. The third was another current board member, whose involvement with the theater went back many years and who had recently come into wealth. At each individual meeting, the interest of each prospect was acknowledged, as was the importance of the project to both the city and the theater. Especially emphasized was the need for a key supporter to take a leadership role in support of the campaign.

● RESULT

After a number of meetings designed to expand the potential donors' vision of the importance of the project and the significance of their involvement in it, success was recorded barely a year after the decision to move ahead had been made. The first prospect agreed to raise his gift to $1 million, from the $500,000 he had previously given, if two other donors could be found to contribute at least $500,000 to the campaign. His challenge was met as the second and third prospects pledged $1 million each. With $3 million in hand, the campaign for the Chicago Shakespeare Theater was officially launched at a groundbreaking ceremony in

September 1998, with nearly half the $12 million goal—later expanded to $13 million—raised. A year later, in October 1999, the theater opened its inaugural season in its new Navy Pier home, a $24 million facility with a state-of-the-art 525-seat courtyard-style theater, a smaller studio theater nearing completion, a resource center for teachers, rehearsal spaces, and a London-style pub. To citywide acclaim, a record subscription audience—up from seventy-two hundred to over sixteen thousand—and a budget that had grown to $4.5 million, the Chicago Shakespeare Theater celebrated its opening with a happy omen. Its funding campaign was directly on schedule.

Chicago Shakespeare Theater's courtyard-style theater. Photography by Ron Solomon © 1999. Reprinted with permission.

QUESTIONS TO ASK

1. Are you prepared to take a giant risk when a unique opportunity presents itself?

2. When you're seeking breakthrough gifts, have you looked internally first?

3. Have you answered every possible question and prepared an unassailable case before approaching your major prospects?

4. Most important, have you conveyed the urgency of your need and your ability to carry through on what you propose?

LESSONS LEARNED

Detailed research will help you identify prime prospects.

LAST WORD

Leadership gifts come from those who believe in your leadership.

The Giving Plan

Reanimating Dormant Planned Giving Programs

BACKGROUND

Before there was a Stephens College in Columbia, Missouri, there was a Columbus Female Academy, founded in 1833, which was succeeded by the Columbia Baptist Female College in 1857. In 1870, Stephens College was officially incorporated. Today, the all-female college of some eight hundred students is perhaps most noted for its programs in the performing arts, especially dance and theater.

○ CHALLENGE

The college did not have an active planned giving program in the 1990s. Although it had accumulated some two hundred planned gifts through 1998, only about 10 percent of the gifts were irrevocable. Moreover, donors had received few follow-up materials, and many names in the prospect files had received little or no attention over the years. With the college set to launch the silent phase of a comprehensive $20 million campaign in 1997, with $5 million of a shadow campaign earmarked as planned giving, the need for a professional approach to planned giving was urgent.

⦿ PLAN

Early in 1998, with funds from a foundation grant, the college activated its planned giving program by hiring a professional to run it, an attorney experienced in running a college planned giving program. As soon as she assumed her position, she systematized the office and looked closely at every existing file, calling or visiting as many prior donors of planned gifts as she could reach during her first weeks on the job. She discovered, interestingly, that her calls resulted in new gifts from people who seemed to have been waiting for someone to contact them. To develop new leads as well as to encourage past givers, letters and brochures were sent to alumni, donors, and prospects, telling them about the new planned giving program at the college. They also were told about a new recognition organization, the Heritage Society, organized for those who had made or would be making planned gifts to the college. To more closely involve members of the society with the concept of planned giving, special events were introduced, beginning with an estate-planning course conducted by a local company. A key part of the subsequent strategy was to recruit as many new members as possible, regardless of their giving level or whether their gift was revocable or irrevocable. In effect, this allowed the college to attract younger alumni with limited resources, who would be able to increase the size of their gifts in subsequent years. Along with confirmation of the receipt of their gifts, donors received personal information forms that included date of birth, so that the college's planned giving professionals could then send them detailed planned giving gift proposals. In addition, the overall focus, reflected in the material appearing in a new quarterly newsletter for society members, was designed to

CPR for Nonprofits

gradually increase recipients' knowledge of the opportunities available to them over a period of time, starting with the most obvious and the easiest to understand—bequests.

● RESULT

The professional approach brought positive results. By November 1999, about eighteen months after the planned giving office had been reactivated, Stephens College was well ahead of the timetable for both the comprehensive campaign and the planned giving phase, the latter resulting in $4 million in gifts. Because of the positive results, the college increased its goal for the overall campaign from $10 million to $30 million.

QUESTIONS TO ASK

1. Have you kept all past donors informed and involved?

2. Have you paid proper attention to all potential donors and not just those at the high end of giving?

3. Have you developed mechanisms to educate prospective donors?

LESSONS LEARNED

There is no magic to planned giving. A working program demands detailed research, a systematic approach, personal involvement with target donors, and a mechanism to provide recognition to donors.

LAST WORD

If a donor has an appetite for giving, it is your job to feed that appetite.

Insider Trading

Sharing Insider Information with Major Donors

BACKGROUND

The World Jewish Congress (WJC) is an international federation of Jewish organizations and communities in over eighty countries throughout the world. Founded in 1936 to mobilize Jewish people against the Nazi terror, the congress has since fought to secure the rights and interests of Jews everywhere.

○ CHALLENGE

A key congress mission has been to aid Holocaust survivors by negotiating with Switzerland to recover assets that had been stolen from them and then deposited in Swiss banks. Although progress had been made, the undertaking was expensive because of extensive research and travel costs. Clearly, there was a need for vastly increased support from the congress's major supporters, the Ambassador's Circle (donors of $1,000 or more). Because there had been few new developments in the months before the appeal to circle members was to be launched (July 1997), the congress decided to focus on past efforts and give direct-mail recipients a unique packet of materials that would draw them into the issue as insiders.

● PLAN

A solicitation packet was created by the WJC's advertising agency, Malchow Adams & Hussey, for mailing in an interdepartmental envelope that would look as if it had been pulled off the WJC shelves and sent just as it was. Opening the packet, the recipient would be made to feel as if he or she were receiving a one-of-a-kind mailing from the WJC files. Included inside, along with a letter from the WJC president, Edgar M. Bronfman, was a plain manila file folder, labeled "Swiss Bank Investigation Developments 3/05/97–5/29/97," which contained a group of highlighted and underlined articles and documents, including several with margin notes. One such note in the margin of a *New York Times* article reporting on the indifference of Swiss bankers until pressures came to bear read, "Pressures spearheaded by WJC." The implication, of course, was that a donor had written this in the margin. Included with the "insiders'" packet was a reply letter to Bronfman from the presumed donor, with the donor's name appearing under "From the Desk of" at the top of the letter. Following the text of the letter, which ends, "As you requested, I have enclosed a tax deductible check or credit card contribution as indicated below," were "handwritten" listings for check or credit card numbers, the amount given, and the donor's signature. Again, the implication was that this was the WJC's checklist for receipt of these donations. Attached to the letter was a Post-it note from EMB (Bronfman) suggesting a specific contribution amount.

● RESULT

The file folder package was sent by stamped first-class mail to 450 Ambassador Circle members at a cost per contact of

From the Desk of
MR. JOHN Q. SAMPLE

Edgar M. Bronfman
President
World Jewish Congress
501 Madison Avenue
New York, NY 10022

Dear Edgar:

I received the letter and file of information you sent to update me on the investigation of Switzerland and its banks.

You have my full support to proceed in assisting the painstaking work of the Volcker Commission as it investigates bank records of ~~~~ ted sums thought to have been depos~~ ~~ring World War II -- and to widen investigation to other countries as e in the matter of lost and looted

Mr. Sample,

If you could make a contribution of $150 today and return it with this note, I would be grateful to you.

-- EMB

~e enclosed a tax-deductible
ution as indicated below.

Sincerely,

Mr. John Q. Sample
123 Main St.
Anytown, US 12345-6789

—— ┬ :_____ Amount :_____

Credit card contribution of $____ :_ VISA
_ MasterCard

Card # :_____ Exp. Date :_____

Signature :_____

99999999   *JQSAMP*

Letter from WJC president Edgar M. Bronfman that accompanied the plain manila file folder. Reprinted with permission.

$34.04. The response rate of 19.6 percent surpassed all expectations. The average gift was $1,261, and contributions totaled $104,000.

QUESTIONS TO ASK

1. Have you explored ways to make your solicitation mailing stand out from other mailings?

2. Have you found ways to make your best donors feel that you are taking them into your confidence and sharing critical organizational information with them?

3. Have you explored ways to personalize your mailings to add to their appeal?

LESSONS LEARNED

You can build a greater sense of involvement with your staunchest supporters by making them feel that you so appreciate their support that you are sharing inside information on a critical issue with them.

LAST WORD

A donor's confidence in your cause grows when you take that donor into your confidence.

CHAPTER FOUR

Involving Your Board and Reaching Your Audiences

THE INTERNAL PUBLICS of a nonprofit organization are vital to its long-term success. Although boards are sometimes vilified as necessary evils by beleaguered organization directors in moments of stress, the personal involvement of the board is integral to the ultimate success of the organization and its mission.

A good working board is a board that works for good—the organization's good, which it will do if it is properly informed and motivated. It also has the capacity, as illustrated in the following cases, to rise to the occasion and meet an organization's most urgent needs with speed and generosity. When push comes to shove, the supportive board is there.

In addition to its financial support, the committed board must be able to recognize and correct its own deficiencies for the overall good of the cause. Quite often, this can be painful, especially if the trustees who have nurtured a group through its formative years must come to terms with their organizational mortality and recognize that it is time for them to pass the torch to others. And just as a board must be aware of gaps within it that need to be filled, so must it be able to defer to a greater good when conducting its business. Board meetings must be run efficiently and democratically. All participants must have the opportunity to contribute, even if that means finding measures that will dramatically and quickly ensure efficiency, as illustrated in some of the following cases.

In addition to the board, there are other internal publics who should play a significant role in an organization's development. To varying degrees, members, volunteers, and those served by the organization must be reached and informed of the organization's program and goals. As the experiences of several of the organizations indicate, although the means of communication may differ, the direct focus of each of these nonprofit organizations is on target for the specific publics for which it is intended.

High Stakes

Involving the Board and Key Supporters at Critical Moments

BACKGROUND

WNYC Radio, founded by New York City in 1924, functioned as a public trust and was the nation's most-listened-to public radio station. Offering a blend of classical music, news, and cultural programming, the station, with a large following of loyal listeners, saw the opportunity to achieve independence by purchasing its licenses from the city.

○ CHALLENGE

In 1997, when WNYC launched its Campaign for Independence, a $20 million drive to purchase its licenses from New York City, it was faced with developing a structure both to raise funds for the license purchase and to support an annual budget that by 1999 would reach $18 million. In 1997, WNYC received a $500,000 two-for-one matching grant from the Corporation for Public Broadcasting, obligating the station to raise $1 million in two years in contributions of $10,000 (or increments thereof) from individuals or family foundations only.

○ PLAN

Of prime importance to WNYC's strategy was the need to directly engage its board of trustees as "fund finders," by having members provide names of potential donors. Solicitation letters signed by the appropriate board member would then be sent to these individuals, requesting an "extraordinary gift" of at least $10,000 toward the license purchase. WNYC also organized a leadership council of supporters at the $500 to $1,000 level to attract potential donors through invitations to special station-focused events. Finally, the station was able to use, as part of its match, contributions of $10,000 or more from individuals who purchased tables at that level for its annual gala, which had been inaugurated in 1998.

● RESULT

Overall, the board response was enthusiastic. Five board members alone, through personal contacts and involvement, generated gifts totaling approximately $400,000. The campaign reached its $1 million goal by the December 31, 1999, deadline with donations from over sixty donors, most at the $10,000 level but several going as high as $60,000. Included in this group were some one dozen first-time donors to the station, several of whom gave $10,000 and gave additional gifts later on.

QUESTIONS TO ASK

1. Have you explored new funding strategies to meet new needs?

CPR for Nonprofits

2. Have you made provisions for explaining unusual or extraordinary requests?

3. Has your board made a total commitment to your campaign?

LESSONS LEARNED

Your board must be able to respond if your need is legitimate, the timing is critical, and the request is reasonable.

LAST WORD

Someone once defined a board as something that is wooden and narrow. But a board can be solid, too, and a solid board that weathers difficult circumstances can be the most important plank in an organization's platform for success.

A Change Is for the Best

Revamping the Board

BACKGROUND

Women in International Security (WIIS) was founded in 1987 by academics at the University of Maryland to increase the influence of women working on foreign and defense affairs. It grew rapidly over the years, increasing membership from one hundred to five hundred in less than a decade, while broadening the scope of its program and its influence on government leaders. Funded primarily by the Ford Foundation, the growth was perhaps a little too rapid, as some of the normal stages in organizational development were bypassed rather than experienced gradually. As one leader put it, "We grew into adulthood without going through adolescence."

○ CHALLENGE

Recognizing the danger of board complacency and burnout, organization leaders approached the Ford Foundation with a three-year regrant proposal, also asking for Ford's help in resolving its organizational growing pains. Ford agreed to a three-year grant of $411,000 in 1996, with the provision that WIIS agree to undergo a detailed professional analysis of its problems.

● PLAN

The Ford grant included $10,000 to pay for a consultant to subject the organization to close scrutiny. WIIS agreed to follow the recommendations made by the consultant. The final report indicated the strong progress that the organization had made, but it also clearly pinpointed a major organizational need—to revamp and revitalize the twenty-three-member board to make it more interactive and strategy oriented and to ensure its ability to create benchmarks to strive for. Following the recommendations laid out to the entire board ten months before board re-elections, WIIS was able to achieve a 50 percent turnover of board members without any rancor or disruption. A few departing trustees, in fact, were so involved with the organization that they asked to join the thirty-five-member advisory board.

● RESULT

A new and revitalized board responded to new responsibilities. Committees began to work on specific tasks and to set short- and long-range goals for themselves. An esprit de corps was clearly evident. A measure of the success can be seen in such developments as WIIS's first fundraising event, participated in fully by board members, which netted over $27,000. In addition, long-range planning took on real meaning, as committees worked to implement large projects in an orderly and structured manner. All activities were prioritized, and several projects that didn't fit into the program were dropped. As organizational efficiency grew, so did the organization. Within several years following restructuring, membership had grown to over a thousand.

QUESTIONS TO ASK

1. Do you have an ongoing board evaluation program?

2. Is your entire board willing to listen to an outside evaluation to determine if you're on the right track?

3. Are you prepared to accept a critical evaluation and act on the suggestions offered?

4. Do you have a plan to measure the effectiveness of operational change?

LESSONS LEARNED

Putting the good of the organization above individual satisfaction is a key to organizational growth. Board members that truly care about the organization they serve must be able to invite criticism, accept it when given, and respond to it when needed.

LAST WORD

Consultants may not know more than you do, but because they come from more than five miles away, they can give you an outside view.

Silence Is Golden– at Times

Raising Big Dollars Before Going Public

BACKGROUND

The Jewish Community Center (JCC) on the Upper West Side was founded in rented quarters in New York City in 1990. Within several years, and without a permanent home, it had grown considerably, with over four hundred different courses and programs in operation and an annual budget of $1.8 million. Its offerings were eclectic and far-reaching, with special programs for virtually every age group and lifestyle in the community. Courses, ranging from single-night sessions to classes that met three, four, or five times over several weeks, included such topics as family health and education, support groups, cultural development, and a wide range of topics for the exploration of Jewish identity and culture. Buoyed by the support the organization had received, its board decided it was ready to take a step that it had considered from the outset—to build its own facility. In 1992, it took an option on a site at 76th Street and Amsterdam Avenue on Manhattan's Upper West Side.

○ CHALLENGE

When the JCC selected an architect in 1995, the time for serious fundraising was at hand. From the beginning, the community served by the JCC was involved in the overall process, including attendance at open houses and meetings. At one such session, the architect discussed the building plans with 110 representatives of the community from all walks of life. The following year, with each of the twenty-five board members and other donors providing all the funding, the center completed the purchase of the land for its new building for $5.3 million.

◑ PLAN

Without an operational development staff and with a $60 million drive looming ahead, the JCC's board reached a key decision: it would hold off formal announcement of a fundraising campaign and raise the needed funds through its own efforts. The following year the center formed a capital campaign council, drawn from within its board and supplemented by key community volunteers, to help organize and move its funding forward and make completion of the full-service eleven-story building a reality by 2001. This group, with the help of friends and center supporters, would help identify potential donors and would then solicit their support and involvement in one-on-one meetings that would stress not merely the JCC's need for a new facility but also how integral a new space was to advancing the vision and values of the organization. That vision, as the JCC identified it, was to become a new model of community organization, one that crossed the broad and varied spectrum of Jewish life and interests.

● RESULT

With executive director, Debby Hirshman, and her staff co-ordinating meeting dates and participants, some seventy individual sessions with potential donors were arranged from 1997 up to the groundbreaking in June 1999 when the fund drive went public. To help present the specific message of the JCC and why the expanded programming emanating from a new building was essential to achieving its mission, Hirshman attended each meeting, along with the board member or supporter responsible for initiating the contact. The results more than met the JCC's expectations, with over 85 percent of the visits resulting in gifts, ranging from $10,000 into the millions. Overall, $36 million was raised, including four gifts over $1 million, and the JCC was easily on target to reach its overall goal. After a $9 million gift was received from the Frederick P. and Sandra Rose Foundation, the building was named the Samuel Priest Rose Building in memory of the donors' son. One key benefit of the drive, according to Hirshman, was that it not only involved those already identified as philanthropists, but it also drew out as supporters a whole new younger generation of donors, who will likely provide support for the center in the years to come.

QUESTIONS TO ASK

1. When planning a major project, have you taken steps to ensure that the board and staff share the same vision?

2. In the process of trying to meet your capital needs, have you emphasized to all your potential supporters not only your capital needs, but even more important your goals and vision?

3. Have you explored a team concept that involves your board and volunteers in a cooperative funding effort?

LESSONS LEARNED

If you can raise a good portion of your needed funding internally, without taking your case to the public, it will help impress potential donors of the significance of your campaign when you do go public.

LAST WORD

In fundraising, the stone from a single slingshot can sometimes do more than a cannon's entire barrage.

CPR for Nonprofits

Red Alert

Keeping Board Meetings on Track

BACKGROUND

The Salisbury-Wicomico Arts Council in Salisbury, Maryland, is a local cultural agency serving some thirty local arts groups. Since its founding in Salisbury in 1967 as Maryland's first arts council, it has promoted local arts activities and has raised consciousness of the significance of the arts to the rural area. Over the years, its board, composed mainly of community leaders, has been an involved and caring group.

○ CHALLENGE

Despite a general harmony among board members, a dynamic was missing from some board meetings. Often some of the members would sit back while more aggressive speakers commanded the floor, often speaking at great length. Clearly, there was a need to involve more board members in the meetings and keep the dialogue on track.

◑ PLAN

The arts council decided on an unusual approach to foster greater participation. Every board member was handed a small red stop sign at each meeting. If at any time a member was speaking at length and another board member thought he or she was speaking excessively, the board member would flash the stop sign, and an immediate informal vote would be taken as to whether the speaker would be allowed to continue or would be forced to stop.

Stop sign used to keep board meetings on track at Salisbury-Wicomico Arts Council. Reprinted with permission.

CPR for Nonprofits

RESULT

Since the plan has been in effect for more than a decade, it has worked wonders, with members deciding if speakers should give up the floor. As a result, trustees have become more conscious of the need to stay on track at meetings. The possibility of blowups by "stopped" speakers has never developed, because the interruptions are always handled with smiles and joking, which defuse potential confrontations.

QUESTIONS TO ASK

1. Do you waste too much time on irrelevant details at board meetings?

2. Are there board members who monopolize the meeting at the expense of others?

3. Are your board meetings so intense that a light moment now and then might not be helpful?

4. Are your board members open to suggestions on how to make each meeting more productive?

LESSONS LEARNED

By using strategies to keep your board meetings business-like, your meetings will stay on track, and you'll be able to focus better on major tasks rather than on minutiae.

LAST WORD

When words fail, sign language may work.

Reader's Choice

Changing Program Formats for Better Results

BACKGROUND

The Allen County Public Library in Fort Wayne, one of Indiana's largest libraries with a main facility and thirteen branches, circulates over four million items a year. Opened in 1895 in the Fort Wayne City Hall, it moved to its present location nine years later and has since developed a large and diverse program serving all age groups.

○ CHALLENGE

To stimulate reading among students in grades six through twelve, the library launched a summer reading program for youngsters in 1994. The eight-week program, which provided incentives, including attendance at special events based on the number of books read, had essentially satisfactory results, although the library staff concluded that the number of participants was not growing at the rate it would like. After examining the program closely and conferring with librarians elsewhere, the library staff concluded that the program, which emphasized the *number* of books read, discouraged participation by slower readers, whose involvement was particularly important.

◐ PLAN

To attract the slower reader without alienating other readers, the library decided to change the format for incentives in 1999. Instead of counting the number of books read, the library changed to counting the time spent reading. Participants who signed up for the program and read for four hours would earn a T-shirt with the program's theme, "Get a clue. . . . Read," printed on it. Participants could then earn a paperback book for every two and a half additional hours spent reading. In addition, by wearing the T-shirt, participants could earn entry to a number of free events held for them, including a laser tag game, a swimming session, and admission to a local minor league baseball game.

● RESULT

The change in format brought immediate results. The number of youngsters signing up for the program increased significantly. So many youngsters became involved that at one of the free incentive events, an evening of bowling, the number of T-shirt wearers wound around the block. The library—quite happily—was forced to schedule another evening for those unable to participate that evening. Actual participation in the program grew from 1,632 to 2,723, and a survey of participants showed that an overwhelming number favored the new format.

QUESTIONS TO ASK

1. Regardless of a program's success, is it reaching every audience you wish to reach?

2. If you're considering changing a program format, how can you make sure that it doesn't do more harm than good?

3. Would a change in format put a heavier burden on the program's financial resources?

LESSONS LEARNED

When a program doesn't work the way you'd like it to work, the problem may not be with the program itself but with the way it's presented. Try a different approach.

LAST WORD

A change doesn't have to be monumental to be monumentally successful.

Reach of Promise

Expanding Programs to Reach Expanding Audiences

BACKGROUND

The Summit Area YMCA was founded in 1886 in Summit, New Jersey. A year later, it moved into its first home in a twenty-five-foot cottage on the second floor of a two-story building, which included a ten-by-twelve-foot gymnasium. It purchased and moved to new quarters in 1888 and bought its current home in 1910, which it occupied in 1912. Today, the Summit Area Y provides one of the most complete multiservice programs in its area, involving more than twenty-five thousand people. Its services, offered through three branches and more than thirty different program sites, include child care, mentoring and tutoring for minority youth, day camping, youth sports, and wellness programs.

○ CHALLENGE

For a number of years, the Y had been running a successful scholarship fund aimed primarily at children from economically disadvantaged families. Annual awards totaled about $35,000. But because of a change in area demographics, with more single-parent families and more impoverished families moving into the area, the Y in 1990 recognized a need to expand its program to include not just children but entire families. A move in this direction would entail far greater promotion of the program and vastly increased funding.

◑ PLAN

At a long-range planning retreat for board and staff members in 1990, the need for a program was discussed in detail, and a plan to meet this new challenge was developed. The two-part plan featured an aggressive promotion campaign to reach every household in the area and an increased and more personalized fund drive. Promotional activity was all encompassing and included new printed materials, mailings, and large lobby posters. Staff involvement in the campaign intensified, heightened by communications-training sessions to enable Y employees to bring the message of the program expansion to Y visitors.

The annual fund campaign, which in past years had relied primarily on telephone contacts, was broadened considerably. To entice larger gifts, the Chairman's Roundtable was created, and members were aggressively recruited. All roundtable members, some fifteen volunteers, were seasoned fundraisers who had worked on the Y's capital fund campaign. In face-to-face meetings, each member made ten to fifteen solicitations, upping the ante from the $50 to $100 suggested in previous campaigns to donations of $500 or more. A new team concept of fund solicitation was also introduced, lessening the burden on individual solicitors.

● RESULT

In the first year after the plan's introduction, the scholarship fund doubled, from $35,000 to $70,000, with many first-time families involved as beneficiaries. Over a ten-year period, the fund has grown by 500 percent, to $175,000, and it is still growing. "The formula worked so well," said Y director Tim Weidman, "that we're still using it."

QUESTIONS TO ASK

1. Even if you have a successful ongoing program, have you asked whether it could be expanded to be even more successful?

2. Have you developed an all-encompassing promotional plan to reach your target audience?

3. Have you trained your entire staff to effectively communicate your message?

LESSONS LEARNED

Every organization faces the dilemma of having a successful program that effectively serves its primary audience but because of changing circumstances may have special relevancy to a new and untapped audience that is difficult to reach. To meet this kind of challenge, an all-encompassing plan that relies heavily on on-target promotion, new funding mechanisms, and personal contact must be carefully developed.

LAST WORD

Change is inevitable. Failure to react to change is irresponsible.

Chicken Crossing?

Getting Members to Read and Respond to Key Messages

BACKGROUND

College unions, which trace their heritage back to medieval times, made their entry on U.S. campuses early in the twentieth century. In 1914, representatives of nine universities in the Midwest came together to form the National Association of Student Unions, which grew over the years to become the Association of College Unions International (ACUI), a worldwide organization representing nine hundred college unions and student activity programs throughout the world, with a total membership of over eighteen hundred.

○ CHALLENGE

With new challenges arising regularly, the organization recognized the need for a strategic plan to help it move into the future. To develop the plan, the executive board, members of a volunteer leadership team, and top staff members spent nearly two years hammering out a document that outlined purpose, values, goals, and strategies for the organization. The plan was completed and passed by the ACUI board in July 1999. Marsha Herman-Betzen, the organization's executive director, then asked its production manager, Kelly Carnahan, to design a strategic plan brochure that could be sent to the entire membership. The completed trifold brochure, which was labeled "Strategic Plan," was attractive, but Herman-Betzen and Carnahan agreed that it was boring and certainly not interesting enough for a recipient to open it and read the plan inside. Clearly, there was a need to find some dramatic or interesting way to get members to open the cover and read the plan.

◑ PLAN

In rethinking the brochure design, they decided to focus on the reasons for developing the plan and to work from there. The core answer that emerged was that the plan would help move the association from point A to point B. Carnahan thought, what better metaphor to use for this than the age-old question, "Why did the chicken cross the road?" That question, printed in white against a dark blue background, became the cover line for the brochure, which then opened to its full length, revealing these other questions:

"How did the chicken know which road to cross?"
"What was the chicken trying to accomplish?"
"What was the chicken thinking?"

Printed below the questions and above the ACUI logo was a statement about the plan, beginning with the line, "So we don't forget what we were thinking as we plot our future path, the Association of College Unions International is pleased to present you with the strategic plan." The folder then opened to reveal the plan inside.

RESULT

The brochure was opened and read. Several members, in fact, indicated that they would never have read the plan had it not been for the compelling concept of the chicken crossing the road. One member thought the approach was so creative that he planned to "steal" it and use the concept for the strategic plan at his university. Perhaps the greatest tribute to the effectiveness of the concept was the noticeable increase in participation in e-mail Listservs set up to discuss the reinvention of the association infrastructures—membership, finance, workforce, governance, and programs and services, including an increase most evident, according to Carnahan, "from people who previously had not participated in the discussion."

QUESTIONS TO ASK

1. Would you open and read your organization's brochure or printed material if you received it cold in the mail?

2. Have you carefully thought out the core message you wish to convey or suggest on your cover or envelope, and is that message clear and unmistakable?

3. Are you willing to depart from the usual and accepted way of conveying information and try a fresh or even offbeat approach?

LESSONS LEARNED

If your message is one that must be heard, make sure that the package in which the message is wrapped will attract attention. You must so pique the interest of recipients that they will want to open it immediately.

LAST WORD

If you ask the right question, everyone will want to know the right answer.

CHAPTER FIVE

Pursuing the Corporate Dollar

NONPROFITS SEEK SUPPORT from corporations for the same reason that the fabled criminal Willie Sutton robbed banks. "That's where the money is," said Sutton. Over the years, however, the corporate presence on the nonprofit scene, though monetarily significant, also has developed in many instances into relationships that go beyond that of giver and getter.

Although direct corporate philanthropy remains a significant source of funding, there has been a decided move by many corporations to seek relationships that satisfy specific corporate goals. For these corporations, sponsorships have become a key part of their marketing and promotion programs. In a prior book, as a way of dramatizing the corporate rationale for funding a project, I quoted another famed American, that pungent and earthy lay philosopher, Mae West, who said, "Goodness has nothing to do with it." Obviously, I was overstating the case to make a point, as many corporate sponsors have a sincere interest in furthering the cause or organization with which they are allied financially. But even though goodness may have a good deal to do with it, sponsorship is a business activity that in addition to its social usefulness usually must meet some sales or marketing objective.

In seeking corporate support, nonprofits have recognized that they have objectives to realize, and the corporation does as well. Therefore, in the best of circumstances, the corporate-nonprofit relationship becomes a partnership, with equal benefits for both parties. The development of a true partnership, as exemplified by the cases that follow, means that the nonprofit organization seeking support has taken the time and the effort to determine that the relationship is a proper and logical match, that it is in good taste, that it is consistent with its image, and that the project to be undertaken is a needed one. As one longtime corporate sponsor, Chase Bank, claims in its promotions, "The right relationship is everything." It is indeed.

Log Cabin Fever

Making Corporate Matches That Fit

BACKGROUND

The National Park Foundation, the official nonprofit partner of the National Park Service, was chartered by Congress in 1967 to support America's National Parks. In addition to other activities, the foundation has been involved in developing many corporate partnerships.

○ CHALLENGE

When it was approached by the marketing agency for Aurora Foods, a company that in its brief four-year history had grown to become a billion-dollar business, the foundation sought to create a partnership with the company that matched corporate needs with a National Park priority project. Interestingly, Aurora, a company that had achieved its growth by acquiring and revitalizing dormant but once popular food brands, was interested in recapturing the audience for its recently acquired Log Cabin Syrup brand, a hundred-year-old product that had not been nationally advertised for years. The foundation identified log cabins in need of help, due to the ravages of time and weather, as a logical match.

❶ PLAN

Aurora, in a direct tie-in to its Log Cabin Syrup brand, partnered with the National Park Foundation to restore historically significant log cabins, beginning in 1998 with the Depression-era Gatekeeper's Cabin at the Grand Canyon. In addition to its pledge of up to $1 million over four years, Aurora also agreed to promote the cabin restoration concept in its advertising and marketing activities for Log Cabin Syrup.

● RESULT

It was clear by its second year that the program, Restoration of America's Log Cabins, was providing a tremendous boost to both partners. During the summer of 1999, the Grand Canyon cabin was fully restored, and renovation work had begun on four log cabins in the Great Smoky Mountains National Park. Aurora Foods also provided funding that year for Junior Ranger programs in eleven National Parks; supported development of educational materials, and programs in the parks; and encouraged public contributions to the campaign through coupons and an on-pack appeal on its newly designed log cabin–shaped bottles. The intensive advertising and promotional campaign included a video news release that generated 18.3 million impressions and extensive print coverage. The partnership, in addition to its many benefits for the National Park Foundation, also helped increase Log Cabin Syrup sales by 16 percent within five months after its introduction, making it the nation's best-selling table syrup brand. The campaign also won a coveted Reggie from the Promotion Marketing Association.

QUESTIONS TO ASK

1. Have you identified your key projects that have the potential for corporate support?

2. Before entering a corporate partnership, have you determined that the relationship is not only logical but also meets a specific organizational need?

3. Do you have a plan to determine exactly how and when you will allocate the resources provided to you?

4. Have you tried to develop a relationship in which your corporate partner and your organization can benefit equally?

LESSONS LEARNED

A partnership that involves an equal commitment from both partners often will result in equal benefits for both partners.

LAST WORD

A common cause can lead to an uncommon return.

The Right Relationship

Developing Sponsor Guidelines

BACKGROUND

The organization that became the National Center for Family Literacy (NCFL) grew out of the Parent and Child Education Program in Kentucky, whose key element was the recognition that the best approach to literacy was through the family, rather than the individual. The Kentucky program, headed by Sharon Darling, was funded by the state legislature beginning in 1986 and so impressed officials of the William R. Kenan Jr. Charitable Trust that it provided a major grant to develop model family literacy programs in both Kentucky and North Carolina. A larger grant from the Kenan Trust in 1989 served to establish the NCFL, headed by Darling, to promote and implement family literacy programs throughout the country.

○ CHALLENGE

The NCFL recognized that nonprofits with nationally recognized programs and strong public images attract the attention of many businesses seeking sponsorships or alliances. Selecting a corporate partner, however, is far from a routine concern, and as the NCFL has learned, nonprofits must think as businesses do before reaching decisions. When the NCFL was approached late in 1997 by the top children's clothing line in the country, OshKosh B'Gosh, which was exploring the possibility of publishing a children's book with the endorsement of the NCFL, the nonprofit organization was intrigued. Over the years, the NCFL had developed partnership guidelines, and it was prepared to think about a proposed relationship in terms of both its long-term compatibility and its potential to substantially boost unrestricted funds and increase public awareness of the program and its goals. It also was prepared to turn down a relationship, regardless of its financial potential, if the match didn't seem a good one. That overall approach had previously led to a successful ongoing one-day-a-year promotion with the QVC television network beginning in 1997, which offers award-winning books for sale. Based on its portion of the proceeds, which it shares with a literacy project in QVC's headquarters area, the NCFL earned over $80,000 in the program's first two years. In discussions with OshKosh's literary consultant, a partnership with that company seemed fruitful as well, and a decision was reached to go far beyond the initial concept. OshKosh would publish a line of children's books aimed at newborns through age six, with the active involvement of the NCFL, which would benefit financially from the arrangement.

◑ PLAN

Preparations continued throughout 1998 to launch a book publication program that would include such classic titles as *The Wizard of Oz* and *Tom Sawyer,* instructional books such as *Counting Is Fun,* and original works, including *Meet Josh and the Doctor,* which featured the OshKosh B'Gosh bear mascot, Josh B'Gosh. All the titles were specifically designed to promote literacy and the joy of reading, and several of the works would feature interactive parent and child activities. The NCFL staff members would help write the books, modifying prose to meet the needs of young-sters and developing interactive activities.

● RESULT

On November 1, 1998, the fifth annual National Family Literacy Day and less than a year since OshKosh had first approached the NCFL, the OshKosh B'Gosh Children's Book Program was officially launched with a first printing of fifteen titles and four hundred thousand books. Under the two-year contract, which includes options for renewal, many more titles are envisioned. The books, which attract-ed widespread attention, were sold in 120 OshKosh B'Gosh stores throughout the country as well as in other children's and toy stores. In the ten months following publication, the NCFL not only had found an effective way to promote reading but also had realized considerable unrestricted in-come from a percentage of each book sold.

QUESTIONS TO ASK

1. Do you have guidelines to help you evaluate business proposals?

2. Do you have staff members who can effectively deal with business on a professional peer-to-peer basis?

SAVE 10 %

off any future purchase
of OshKosh B'Gosh
children's books

Only valid at OshKosh B'Gosh
company-owned stores.
Not valid with any other offer
or on prior purchases.
Offer void where prohibited.
Offer expires 12/31/99.

OSHKOSH
B'gosh
THE GENUINE ARTICLE

www.oshkoshbgosh.com

**Teach the parent.
Reach the child.**

The OshKosh B'Gosh
children's book program
is endorsed by the nation's
leading family literacy
organization. Since 1989,
the National Center for
Family Literacy (NCFL) has
helped thousands of families
to become self-sufficient by
offering programs that
combine early childhood
education, adult literacy
education, parent support,
and structured interaction
between parents and their
children. Support the power
of family literacy and give
the gift of reading.

**NATIONAL CENTER FOR
FAMILY LITERACY**
www.famlit.org

National Center for Family Literacy bookmark (two sides). Reprinted with permission.

3. Can you look objectively at each proposal and if necessary, say no?

LESSONS LEARNED

A potential corporate partnership must be recognized as just that, a potential. Instead of becoming so intrigued by the prospect of additional funding or major promotional help, each organization must place itself in the driver's seat and determine if the match is logical, if it is in good taste, if it meets a specific need, and if the nonprofit organization is getting as much as it is giving.

LAST WORD

Although a nonprofit organization isn't a business, it must be managed in a businesslike manner.

In Union There Are Sponsorships

Boosting Sponsorship Through Partnerships

BACKGROUND

Aquariums, although small in number when compared with zoos, are resources of growing significance to their communities. Like many of their cultural counterparts, they require sponsorship as a key area of support, especially by companies with sea-related products or services.

○ CHALLENGE

When seven leading aquariums became aware that each had signed a separate three-year sponsorship agreement with Tetra, a company that markets fish food, they realized that they shared a common resource and a potent marketing tool. Although most of the institutions had a regional image, they knew that if they came together in a partnership and combined their resources, they could create a cause-related program that could be activated nationally and would be very attractive to national sponsors. Although a number of people cautioned against a sponsorship partnership, arguing that the institutions had different needs and different agendas, the decision to go ahead was unanimous. The participating institutions were the New Orleans Aquarium of the Americas, Tampa's Florida Aquarium, Baltimore's National Aquarium, Boston's New England Aquarium, Chicago's John G. Shedd Aquarium, Chattanooga's Tennessee Aquarium, and Corpus Christi's Texas State Aquarium.

◑ PLAN

After meeting early in 1998, the seven organizations joined to form the Aquarium Alliance that summer, basing its structure on a business plan that outlined mission, goals, policies, and financial matters. Drawing on the sponsorship agreements with Tetra, the plan involved shared benefits for each of the partners, with 25 to 30 percent of each agreement divided equally. According to the formula they devised, the remaining funds were to be divided each year, with each aquarium receiving an amount equivalent to its percentage of the total attendance of all alliance institutional members that year. To ensure a professional and objective approach, and to maximize its opportunities, the alliance hired an agency on a percentage basis to solicit potential sponsors.

● RESULT

Within months of creating the alliance, the first national sponsor was confirmed. Yahoo!, the Internet company, signed a three-year agreement for in-kind services at an estimated $1 million a year. Although many other sponsorships were in the process of being developed, and all of the aquariums' corporate sponsorship officials were impressed with the progress that had been made, the alliance recognized that in order to move ahead there was a need for a more formalized arrangement and an organizational infrastructure. In August 1999, the chief financial officers and senior marketing staff of each of the aquariums came together in Chicago to discuss developments to date, more clearly define roles and relationships, and set up a more structured organization and rotating leadership arrangement. In addition, the alliance decided that it was critical to its success to hire a contractual sponsorship fulfillment manager, not only to coordinate benefit fulfillments but also to ensure seamless communications among the partners. More confident than ever of success, the alliance issued a paper, which it circulated to its members, outlining the new organizational structure and format for procedures. In late 1999, the alliance's sponsorship sales agency redirected its efforts to focus on international initiatives.

QUESTIONS TO ASK

1. Are there organizations in your sphere of activity that might share a common need and might have the potential to partner with you to help meet that need?

2. If you're involved in a partnership, have you made sure all partnership participants clearly understand their commitments and responsibilities?

3. Have the CEO, board, and senior marketing staff bought into the partnership?

4. Have you stopped at various junctures to make sure that all issues have been discussed and resolved?

LESSONS LEARNED

Even when needs are different, involvement in a common cause, when carefully structured and developed in cooperation with organizations that have similar programs, can lead to mutual benefits.

LAST WORD

A partnership can make beautiful music when every partner dances to the same tune.

To Market We Will Go

Replacing Lost Corporate Sponsors

BACKGROUND

The Louisiana Children's Museum has been educating and entertaining New Orleans youngsters since its founding in 1981. One of its major attractions for more than a decade had been an exhibit sponsored by a local supermarket: a one-room grocery store, scaled to the size of children, lined with shelves of pretend food items, including produce and seafood. The checkout counter featured an old-fashioned cash register.

○ CHALLENGE

In 1999, the grocery store exhibit's sponsor went out of business. Facing a loss of support, the museum knew that it had to find a new sponsor as soon as possible.

◐ PLAN

Moving quickly, the museum developed a plan to find a replacement. Cataloging its needs and strengths, the museum, within several weeks, prepared a list of potential sponsors who met its criteria and sent out requests for proposals (RFPs) to each of the companies on its list. The RFP outlined details on the exhibit and data on its attendees, the specific kind of partnership the museum was seeking, and the benefits to the sponsor. The museum stressed its interest in finding not just funding support but a true partner for three consecutive years. The partner would help advance the museum's efforts to promote participatory learning and would help the museum with advertising, promotion, and volunteer support. Sent to four carefully selected supermarkets, the RFP, designed to attract only those companies that met its criteria, resulted in responses from three and presentations by two of them.

● RESULT

The presentation by the A&P's Sav-A-Center, which had recently purchased seven stores in the greater New Orleans area, met the guidelines set by the museum, emphasizing its desire to "establish a community partnership that reflects our commitment to quality and to children." Less than six months after the museum learned of the loss of its former sponsor, Sav-A-Center agreed to become the official three-year sponsor of the exhibit, with the right to renew. Sav-A-Center immediately set in motion plans to renovate the exhibit at a cost of over $80,000. Sav-A-Center's total commitment over three years, including renovation and maintenance, was over $425,000, a significantly higher sum than the previous sponsor had paid. Other aspects of the agreement included annual sponsorship at $20,000 a year, the hiring of a public relations professional to work with museum staff to promote the exhibit at $12,000 a year, and annual in-kind product, advertising, and promotional support at $75,000 a year. This included a range

Sav-A-Center food pyramid, magnet, and grocery list on the following page reprinted with permission.

of cross promotions, museum ticket sales at Sav-A-Center stores, register coupons, museum tag lines in store print ads, and volunteer support for the museum. In January 2000, the new exhibit was officially unveiled in a special ceremony.

QUESTIONS TO ASK

1. Even if you have a sponsor for a specific activity or program, are you prepared to move quickly if you unexpectedly lose that sponsor?

2. Do your RFPs include, in addition to sponsor benefits, a careful delineation of the specific kind of relationship you are seeking?

3. Have you assembled personnel who are professionally equipped to evaluate any proposals that you receive?

LESSONS LEARNED

A replacement for any kind of loss can be found only if you develop a plan that carefully assesses your needs, your strengths, and the specific kind of replacement you are seeking and only if you deal from your strength and do not compromise your worth.

LAST WORD

If you plan well, today's loss could become tomorrow's gain.

Points of Sale

Developing Beneficial Corporate Partnerships

BACKGROUND

Although there has been a symphony orchestra in Calgary, Alberta, Canada, since 1910, two world wars interrupted orchestra development, and it was not until 1955 that the current Calgary Philharmonic Orchestra was formed. It moved into the new Jack Singer Concert Hall in 1985. In addition to presenting its own program each season, the versatile Philharmonic also serves as the orchestra for the Calgary Opera and the Alberta Ballet. It performs before over a hundred thousand people in Calgary each season. Because Calgary is the second largest corporate headquarters base in Canada, after Toronto, area businesses have related to the orchestra's success and have been strong supporters of its activities over the years.

○ CHALLENGE

Nourished by an atmosphere of corporate involvement, the orchestra has not been unaccustomed to partnership suggestions made by business. One such offer of involvement was made in 1994 by John Torode, the head of Torode Realty, a leading real estate firm in Alberta. Torode approached Leonard Stone, then executive director of the orchestra, asking how he could help the orchestra. With funding an obvious need, Torode wondered if through his firm, which leased properties throughout the province, some kind of plan might be developed to raise funds for the orchestra.

◑ PLAN

In cooperation with Stone and the symphony staff, Torode worked out an unusual arrangement that involved not only a commitment on the part of Torode's firm but an equal commitment by every member of his sales force. For every square foot of real estate leased by Torode Realty in Calgary and Edmonton that year, 10 cents would be contributed to the orchestra, with half coming from the firm and the other half coming from the salesperson making the sale. Convinced that the promotion would attract public attention and give them a competitive edge and pleased to contribute to the community, the sales force agreed to the concept. Torode set his sights high, aiming to lease one million square feet that year, which would result in a $100,000 gift to the symphony. To heighten awareness of the unique campaign, Torode gave symphony tickets to every property leaser so the buyer could attend a symphony concert with the salesperson who consummated the deal.

● RESULT

The concept, promoted by both the orchestra and the realty firm, exceeded expectations. By the end of the year, Torode Realty had achieved record sales, leasing 1,800,000 square feet, resulting in a gift of $108,000 to the symphony. In addition to the sales results, Torode derived other benefits. As a result of his support for the orchestra, his firm won both national and local business-in-the-arts awards. The campaign had a further benefit. Torode joined the symphony board the following year, served for three years, and became a key supporter as well as event sponsor. "We were so blown away by his largesse," said Stone, "that we expressed our appreciation with a private evening concert featuring Skitch Henderson."

QUESTIONS TO ASK

1. When a business says it's interested in helping you, are you prepared to help them help themselves while they're helping you?

2. Have you developed a plan to promote a business help concept?

3. Have you found a proper way to thank a key supporter?

LESSONS LEARNED

When a corporate sponsor comes to you with an offer of help, take the time to develop with that sponsor the kind of sponsorship that not only will help your bottom line but also will help promote the sponsor's key activities.

LAST WORD

When a gift horse comes your way, ride it.

CHAPTER SIX

Employing a Businesslike Approach

THE BUSINESS of running a nonprofit organization is a complex one. Because mission supersedes profit as the motivating operational force, unearned income through donations, project grants, and special events must be raised to supplement the ongoing activities that provide an organization's income base.

While focusing on strengthening their comprehensive development programs and their ongoing income-producing activities, many nonprofit organizations, including some that subsidize many of their own activities, must find ways to operate as efficiently and as economically as they can. Within the fragile economic framework that many organizations operate, there is little room for waste. In fact, it might be said that in fund management many nonprofits could teach their profit-making brethren a lesson or two.

In the examples that follow, efficiency and sound business judgment are epitomized. Whether finding ways to drastically cut costs without jeopardizing the organizational effort or coming up with a new approach to develop a needed facility, organizations have found cost-efficient cooperative approaches that work. They also have been successful in the especially demanding task of developing new income-producing activities from the ground up that in addition to their financial benefits also promote and further the organizational mission.

Perhaps the key lesson to be learned from these examples is that although a nonprofit organization is not a business, it must be run in a businesslike manner, boosted of course by the kind of compassion and zeal that belief in a cause can engender.

Doing It Your Way

Taking On Challenging Programs

BACKGROUND

The Global Fund for Children was founded in Durham, North Carolina, in 1993—it has since moved to Washington, D.C.—by Maya Ajmera to promote the cause of human rights for children throughout the world. Ajmera, who was then a recent graduate of Duke University, came up with the idea of creating and selling a product that not only would earn revenue income for the organization but also would effectively become an innovative communication tool to promote its message. She wanted to create the kind of books for children that she believed did not then exist—books that would entertain, educate, and advance the organization's message. Her research on potential funding sources led her to the Echoing Green Foundation, where she was able to make a persuasive case for seed money, winning $75,000 over three years to get the organization on its feet.

○ CHALLENGE

Ajmera coauthored the first work, *Children from Australia to Zimbabwe,* a book with pictures that promoted multiculturalism and presented a positive image of children.

Focusing on the things that tie children together, the organization wished to publish the book under its own imprint, Shakti, after the Hindu goddess personifying strength and wisdom. The book, however, was rejected by every publisher to whom it was sent.

◑ PLAN

Without a publisher, the fund reached a critical decision—it would self-publish the book. Needing $60,000 to get the book in print, the fund approached support sources in North Carolina, where it was then based. All funders were promised that if they provided needed support, every public school in North Carolina would get three copies of the book. By 1996, after money had trickled in from many different sources, the fund published seven thousand copies of the book, with a foreword by Marian Wright Edelman, president of the Children's Defense Fund.

● RESULT

The book created a stir, and copies not earmarked for schools were sold to a local distributor. When news of its success reached the publishing world, several of the same publishers who had rejected the title initially came back to the Global Fund for Children, seeking to become involved. Looking for a new role as a creative developer rather than a publisher—the role it was forced to take to sell its first book—the fund searched for a company that would best meet its needs. That company was Charlesbridge Publishing in Boston, which presented a plan that used the fund's own publishing imprint, Shakti for Children, and awarded a royalty payment of 15 to 20 percent, much higher than the usual royalty. The new line that resulted from the alliance, with five titles and forewords by such notables as John Hope Franklin and Bill Bradley, had great success. *Children from Australia to Zimbabwe* alone sold twenty-five thousand copies and won two national book awards. As a result of this success, the fund has brought its name and message to a larger audience than it had anticipated, and it has been able to forge relationships and partnerships with other organizations to promote its message. In addition, it was able to use a portion of its royalties to make grants of up to $5,000 each to innovative programs that support underserved children in Pakistan, Uganda, Brazil, and India.

QUESTIONS TO ASK

1. If you have a viable project essential to your mission, have you developed as complete a list of options as possible and fully explored each of them?

2. If your project does not win acceptance, and you believe in it, are you prepared to develop that project yourself?

3. Once you have realized your objective, do you have a plan to keep moving ahead?

LESSONS LEARNED

If you have faith in your concept and see a project as essential to fulfillment of your mission, use every avenue of research available to come up with potential support sources, and use every contact you already have and new ones you can develop to move that project beyond the idea phase into an action mode.

LAST WORD

Rejection doesn't always mean failure. It merely means that you may have to find an alternative route to success.

Cheaper by the Dozen

Cutting Costs Through Cooperative Activities

BACKGROUND

The White Plains Hospital Center in White Plains, New York, is one of the largest and most respected community hospitals in New York's Westchester County. Established in 1893, the center, with a budget of $115 million, serves well over 130,000 patients a year. Included among its resources is operation of the $8.5 million Dickstein Cancer Treatment Center. Opened in 1999, this cancer facility is the county's only freestanding building devoted solely to cancer care and is its most comprehensive facility for the diagnosis and treatment of cancer.

○ CHALLENGE

As the health care field has undergone major changes in recent years, the hospital center, along with other institutions in its field, has been besieged with entreaties to align itself with prestigious academic medical centers that could expand its scope of operations. Determined to retain its independence and its own identity as a local health resource, which it had cultivated over the years, the center nonetheless was afflicted with a malady common to its field, the growing cost of purchased goods and services. There was a clear need for the center to find a way to cut its costs while maintaining its independence.

◑ PLAN

After considering many options, the center decided that a cooperative purchasing program in alliance with other area hospitals could help it reduce costs without in any way threatening its independence or identity. With a cooperative in mind, it began to approach other independent community-based hospitals in the county that were known for the quality of their patient care services. A key concern in selecting partners was their willingness to work in collaboration with other hospitals who traditionally were considered their competitors. In 1996, the White Plains Hospital Center joined forces with Mount Kisco's Northern Westchester Hospital Center to form HealthStar, a joint purchasing agency, which added two other county hospitals within the next few months—Sleepy Hollow's Phelps Memorial Hospital Center and Bronxville's Lawrence Hospital. Each participating hospital was asked to contribute a $3 million start-up fee as an indication of its commitment to help the new HealthStar cooperative become operational. Designed as a combined business resource, HealthStar was structured to act both as a purchasing agent, buying everything from food to health equipment to drugs to business machines, and as a management network, negotiating managed-care contracts. In its operation, HealthStar, the parent company that oversees the four independent hospitals participating in the program, has an active board of directors. The CEO of each of the hospitals serves on the board, and together they act as a management team, meeting biweekly to chart the cooperative's course. The daily management and co-ordination of HealthStar operations is in the hands of a senior management workforce.

● RESULT

The partnership has proved its effectiveness several times over. By combining their forces and purchasing in bulk, the hospitals have achieved substantial savings on purchases in virtually every area of hospital activity. The White Plains Hospital Center alone, which has successfully resisted alliances that might have threatened its independence, has not only maintained its identity but during the partnership's first three years has saved $5.2 million as a result of the arrangement.

QUESTIONS TO ASK

1. Before entering a partnership, have you determined what specific needs that partnership will meet?

2. Is there compatibility in method of operation, needs, and similarity of services?

3. Do you have an operational plan that will ensure professional management?

LESSONS LEARNED

Developing and maintaining an identity is a key concern for many institutions. An institution's identity need not be sacrificed in a cooperative program, however, if the purpose of the relationship is to achieve a specific goal that is mutually beneficial and if each of the participants understands and is committed to the parameters of the relationship.

LAST WORD

Cooperation among competitors can lead to financial harmony.

Sweet Buy and Buy

Developing Mail Order Businesses

BACKGROUND

Community Workshop, Inc. (CWI), in Glens Falls, New York, has been providing a wide range of services to individuals with disabilities residing in three northeast New York counties since its founding in 1963. With services ranging from family support activities to day treatment to a full range of employment services, CWI had been expanding its agenda to meet the growing needs of the audience it serves.

○ CHALLENGE

Almost entirely funded by state grant money, the organization recognized that with cutbacks in state government support its program would be endangered. Clearly, there was a need to expand Community Workshop's funding horizons and find a creative way to achieve self-sufficiency. In December 1997, CWI's management and board, along with local community leaders, came together to brainstorm about the possible business ventures that CWI might undertake to significantly boost its income. A range of ideas was considered before a consensus was reached. CWI's home base is in Glens Falls, which is in the Adirondacks mountain range. It was thought that a focus on the area, through the sale of well-crafted Adirondack-made products, would not only be fitting but would also help support and promote the community and area craftspeople.

◐ PLAN

Recognizing that it would have to invest its own funds to purchase inventory, CWI decided to bring in an outside expert with a fresh point of view to help develop a business plan and move the project forward. Early in 1998, based on recommendations from its board, CWI brought in a Pennsylvania consulting firm, which worked with CWI staff over the following months to develop a format for a new mail order catalog business featuring Adirondack products. A key early recommendation of the firm was that CWI hire a person with a catalog background to manage the operation. In a stroke of serendipity, a woman with the precise background needed had recently relocated to the Glens Falls area. Hired in March as catalog sales manager, Nancy Busch, along with selected staff members, began to work on a tight timetable, combing the local area for catalog merchandise. Armed with sample products, Busch and her team met with focus groups in April—one in New York City and one in Connecticut—to get their input on items to be offered for sale. Treating the operation as a business, albeit one run by a nonprofit entity, CWI took out a loan from a local bank, rather than seeking funding, to cover the cost of inventory purchases, catalog design, printing, and mailing. By May, the selection of merchandise was finalized and by August the catalog was completed. In mid-September 1998, after setting up a computer database system and a separate order response division and call center for overflow calls, the first copies of *The Pack Basket: A Mountain Classics Catalog* were sent to a list of 150,000 people, most of them names from rented lists of catalog merchandise buyers.

● RESULT

The results of the first mailing exceeded all goals, meeting benchmarks along the way and achieving a response rate of 1 percent. Although catalog businesses usually take five to eight years to establish themselves and operate profitably, *The Pack Basket* had become a regular fixture of the CWI operation by fall 1999, with two separate catalogs published each year. With its own Web site and a growing number of customers, as well as satisfied manufacturers, CWI has expanded its inventory to include more substantial items, including a number of articles made outside the Adirondack area. Eventually, Community Workshop hopes to employ individuals with disabilities—its own clients—in *The Pack Basket* operation.

QUESTIONS TO ASK

1. If you're considering a business venture, have you made sure that you have a carefully developed business plan before you move ahead, that your business plan isn't too aggressive or unrealistic, and that the consultant you hire to help develop your plan is knowledgeable not just in business but also in the type of business you wish to pursue?

The Pack Basket Catalog brings mail order income to Community Workshop, Inc. Reprinted with permission.

2. If you must finance a new business operation, have you explored all funding options before deciding which way to go, being aware that many philanthropic funders might consider a business operation too complex to support?

3. Will you operate on a scope that fits within your budget and capabilities, and will you have the resources to sustain a business until it can sustain itself?

LESSONS LEARNED

Developing a new business means reliance on a carefully structured business plan, attention to details, and involvement of a professional manager.

LAST WORD

If you're going to operate a business, act like a business.

Thought for Food

Getting People You Help to Help You

BACKGROUND

The Good Shepherd Food Bank in Lewiston, Maine, has been collecting food and distributing it to local food banks since 1981. Serving a handful of local groups at first, it has since expanded to serve nearly four hundred food banks throughout the state. As the need for its service increased over the years, the strain on its resources also grew.

○ CHALLENGE

By the mid-1990s, the food bank recognized the serious situation it faced: it was running out of storage space. In 1997, when the food bank had to refuse an estimated three million pounds of food a year because its warehouse was too small, it knew that the time for action had come. Clearly, there was a need to undertake a first-time capital campaign to enlarge its warehouse.

◑ PLAN

Although the initial concept was to raise about $1 million for warehouse enlargement, it soon became apparent that even more space was needed. With the help of consultant William Kruger of Tucson's Capital Quests, the capital campaign, which begin in 1997, was restructured to encompass construction of a second facility in Bangor, a hundred miles away. This was to make distribution easier while also providing significantly more space. In developing a strategy, they agreed that initial support should come from agencies served by Good Shepherd, who would recognize that the campaign would also be helping them. As Good Shepherd's executive director, JoAnn Pike stated, "If those agencies didn't recognize the need, then nobody would." In a unique concept, leaders of every agency served by Good Shepherd were invited to breakfast, lunch, or dinner over a four-day period in May 1998 at one of eight different sites in the state. They were shown a video about the need for the enlarged facilities, so they would learn about the importance of the project to them and the need for their support. The whirlwind activity, which cost Good Shepherd $4,000, drew some one thousand attendees, who were asked to send letters of endorsement indicating how Good Shepherd's activities helped their respective organizations achieve their missions. They also were asked to support the campaign, with suggested donations of $200 a year for three years.

● RESULT

The response was positive. Endorsement letters poured into Good Shepherd's offices. Agencies that had attended the meals contributed $100,000 to the campaign, with gifts averaging $1,000 and with several in the $5,000 range. The letters proved essential to the public phase of the campaign and helped open doors throughout the state. One key official, a banker who headed a group of community banks in the state, was so excited about the program that he promoted the campaign to his colleagues. This resulted in meetings between leaders of Good Shepherd and the presidents of virtually every bank in the state, who wanted to know more about what was being done in their communities. For the first time in eighteen years, the state's governor visited a food bank. Within a year of the luncheons, the campaign had nearly reached its goal, raising almost $1.5 million, including a $250,000 challenge grant from the Stephen and Tabitha King Foundation.

QUESTIONS TO ASK

1. When you explore all potential funding sources, do you include those closest to you?

2. Have you developed a vehicle to reach and inform your closest audiences of your needs, and have you determined how they can help themselves by helping you?

3. Have you developed a follow-up plan to market the opportunities you reap?

LESSONS LEARNED

Don't hesitate to ask those who rely most on your help to help you, especially if you can find ways to show them what they can gain from helping you.

LAST WORD

There may come a time when you ask not what you can do for others, but what others can do for you.

The Yearn to Earn

Developing Earned Income Programs

BACKGROUND

In 1947, Bernard Ross, a practicing physician in New York City, purchased a seventy-five-acre dairy farm, Green Chimneys, in what was then rural Putnam County, as a gift for his son Samuel. A junior at the University of Virginia, Samuel had evinced a strong interest in operating a year-round school and camp for young children whose parents were in need of out-of-home care for them. After a year's conversion of the farm, timed to coincide with Samuel's college graduation, Green Chimneys took in eleven children in the summer of 1948 as its residents for the first summer. The program kept growing, and now, in addition to its main campus in Brewster, Green Chimneys has ongoing programs in Danbury, Connecticut; in Bedford, Ossining, and Hawthorne, New York; and in New York City. Green Chimneys is now a $20 million operation, serving about two hundred learning disabled and emotionally disturbed youngsters in residence and over a thousand more through its ongoing services.

○ CHALLENGE

Green Chimneys relied on private and government grants to meet its annual $20 million budget. A key aspect of its program focused on finding ways to involve its resident population in meaningful activities that were both challenging and personally rewarding. Because residential programs often incur deficits, administrators decided that Green Chimneys had to find a way to meet its program needs while at the same time offsetting its costs.

◐ PLAN

Green Chimneys's staff, headed by Samuel Ross, its managing director, recognized that many of the activities that would serve residents could, if properly structured, also bring in needed income. Although many activities had been undertaken in the past, a plan was developed to structure new activities to achieve the dual purpose of supporting the mission and raising needed income. To achieve these goals, business feasibility studies had to be developed to test the viability of potential projects as well as attractive marketing campaigns to promote them. Included among the many activities considered were beekeeping, a greenhouse and garden, a poultry farm, a café, a catering service, and a moveable farm.

● RESULT

The activities developed by Green Chimneys have more than met their goals. Not only have residents enriched their skills and boosted their confidence in such varied roles as farmers, beekeepers, and waiters, while earning money at the same time, but the projects have proved economically successful. Sales of products produced at the resident farm in Brewster, New York, such as organic eggs and honey, have been excellent. Activities such as "farm-on-the-moo-ve," which transports animals and their resident caretakers to area schools, have proved especially rewarding. Success also has led to publicity, which has attracted the notice of both visitors and funding sources and has encouraged Green Chimneys to develop such sponsor-supported attention-getting programs as a weeklong Little Folks Days and Birds of Prey Day. The Brewster farm now draws twenty thousand visitors a year, many of them fee-paying guests, who also contribute to donation boxes. Green Chimneys has won plaudits from around the world, enriched the capabilities of its clients, and attracted new support from foundations, corporations, and individual donors. It also has been able to earn about $500,000 a year from its mission-related programs.

QUESTIONS TO ASK

1. Do planned mission-related activities fit your raison d'être?

2. Have you pretested each of the planned activities to ensure that they are viable and sustainable and that they have the potential to be financially rewarding?

3. Do you have the staff, capabilities, and resources to undertake these activities without endangering other aspects of your overall program?

LESSONS LEARNED

An earned income program that relates directly to your mission and serves your constituency is much more meaningful in the long run than a program that bears little relationship to your stated purposes, even if it is more lucrative financially.

LAST WORD

By serving your mission, you can serve other key needs as well.

CHAPTER SEVEN

Maximizing Your Grassroots Potential

THE TERM *grass roots* is most frequently used to designate areas and activities removed from the mainstream or small in size. Geographically, it might refer to rural areas or small towns. In the context of this chapter, *grass roots* is broadly applied in a geographical sense to some areas and activities far from our usual perspective.

It is another context, however, that provides the linkage among the activities cited. In each of these cases, the challenges to be met were new ones, in several instances as new as starting an entire program or concept from scratch. A first-time fund drive, a first-time attempt to capture a target audience, or a first-time undertaking designed to involve an entire community in a unified effort all had a similar base and starting point. In each of these instances, the leaders involved in the effort recognized that the question they faced was not if they could get started but how and when they could get started.

The will to succeed, by itself, does not guarantee success. But when that will is fortified by commitment, unrelenting effort, and a discerning plan of action that recognizes its own boundaries and limitations, then success may soon be within reach.

Closer Than You Think

Soliciting Funds from Program Participants

BACKGROUND

The Omega Institute for Holistic Studies, a nonreligious retreat, grew out of a spiritual community in Lebanon Springs, New York, in 1977. Organized to develop an interdisciplinary learning center for the cross-pollination of ideas, the program operated for its first few years in rented facilities, where it presented some thirty to fifty weekend to weeklong programs each summer. In 1982, the institute took a step forward by purchasing a property in Rhinebeck, New York, as its new center. Since then, the institute has grown considerably, presenting some three hundred on-site programs for over twelve thousand people each year during the April-to-October season at its Rhinebeck campus, as well as running conferences and programs around the country. As stated in one of its publications, Omega has, through its programs, "helped usher in to American society holistic health, wellness and healing; world spirituality; and cross-cultural music and art. We have also helped introduce new advances in a wide variety of important issues, including relationships and family healing, aging and death and dying work, and environmental and societal renewal."

○ CHALLENGE

Over the years, Omega had financed its activities, which focus on personal growth and healing, primarily through earned income, the fees it received from people who attended its three- to five-day programs. In an attempt to create a link to its spiritual roots, Omega wanted to build a sanctuary on its grounds, where attendees could pause to reflect and pray in any way they wished. Never having done any serious fundraising before, Omega was faced with a need for $200,000 to build the sanctuary. It was willing to put up $100,000 from its own resources, but because there was no existing development program, it didn't know how to raise the additional $100,000.

◑ PLAN

Omega leaders decided that because this was something so germane to its mission, it would rely on its program participants, but in a low-key effort consistent with its overall approach. "If we can't raise funds for this from our supporters, then we can't raise funds period," said one of the leaders. The approach that developed was aimed at the program participants, the two groups of from two hundred to four hundred different people who visited the retreat every week. It was decided that at the opening orientation session for the visitors, an Omega leader would discuss the retreat for a few minutes, indicating its significance to the overall Omega program. Then at some point during a group's stay, a walk in silence would be taken to the sanctuary site, where a faculty member would recite a nondenominational prayer, blessing the land and the site. This would be followed by an open invitation to any participant to say whatever he or she wished. Several weeks after the visit, all participants would receive low-key letters describing the goal for the sanctuary and soliciting their support.

● RESULT

In less than a year, the $100,000 was raised without Omega having to resort to any other fundraising strategies. A year later, when Omega leaders decided it would be in the spirit of their program to have a hermitage—a house for visiting speakers—a similar approach was used. In this case, however, participants who walked to the site of the proposed hermitage were asked to reflect and then place a stone on the altar to mark that they had been there. In a matter of months, the altar was running over with stones, and Omega was running over with money.

QUESTIONS TO ASK

1. For a major first-time fund drive, have you communicated the importance of your need to your primary constituency?

2. While remaining consistent with your image, have you found some interesting, or even dramatic, way to focus your constituents' attention specifically on your needs?

3. Once you've completed a successful drive, have you gone back to your supporters to ask their help to meet still another need?

LESSONS LEARNED

When you're launching a major fund drive for the first time, look first at those individuals who have already benefited from your program. Although your approach to them need not be strident or aggressive, you must emphasize your need and why it is important to you in a tone consistent with your image.

LAST WORD

If you don't ask, someone else will.

Think Small

Merging Expertise
with Local Enthusiasm

BACKGROUND

The Siyoka Secondary School serves its community of West Nicholson, in the Matabeland South region of Zimbabwe, as a social as well as an educational resource. In an area where educational needs are great, its facilities, especially its library, benefit not only its young students but also the area's adult population.

○ CHALLENGE

When leaders of the secondary school recognized a need for a new community library, they knew that it would be difficult to find the funds to build the facility. Since fundraising isn't an everyday activity in Zimbabwe, especially in a rural area such as West Nicholson, the community turned to someone for assistance who presumably had the know-how to help them find the money—American Peace Corps worker Rosemary Kugler. Although not a fundraiser by background or training, Kugler recognized that total community involvement would be the key to the success of any campaign.

❶ PLAN

Early in 1997, Kugler organized a library committee of local parents, teachers, religious leaders, and political figures. After an initial meeting to plan its activities, elect officers, and establish a banking account for the library, the group met regularly every month. With guidance from Kugler, they outlined a local fundraising program to be introduced over the coming months, beginning with a community festival focusing on the need for a new library. This was followed by a series of raffles and later, after a number of months, a two-day sponsored walk. The walk, which called on every resource in the community, resulted in small pledges from an increasingly enthusiastic community and a pledge of enough free cement, valued at $4,000, from one contractor to construct the building. Kugler and her committee then wrote a successful proposal to United States Aid in Development to fund the purchase of metal shelves for the existing library, which later could be transferred to the new library when it was completed. Having demonstrated local support for the project, the committee, which had raised about $7,000 in an eighteen-month period, decided it was ready to find the remaining funds to build the library. Under Kugler's guidance, a major grant proposal to buy all the building materials needed was submitted to some dozen foreign embassies in Zimbabwe. The proposal, which stressed local commitment to the project, indicated that the community itself would provide the labor and the construction supervisor to build the library.

● RESULT

In December 1998, the committee received a grant of approximately $10,000 from the British High Commission in Zimbabwe to fund the purchase of building materials for the community library. In June 1999, several months after Kugler had returned to the states (she turned the project over to her successor in West Nicholson), the community began to build its new library.

QUESTIONS TO ASK

1. In organizing a community fundraising effort, have local leaders been identified and recruited?

2. Have activities been planned that a community not used to raising funds has the ability to undertake?

3. Has there been a strong demonstration of local support before outside funding is sought?

LESSONS LEARNED

With a little direction, total community involvement, and appropriate events, a grassroots funding effort can impress larger funding sources with the importance of a project and with the local commitment to it.

LAST WORD

In an all-out community fund drive, the community must be all in.

Game, Set, Match

Turning Funding
Concepts into Reality

BACKGROUND

In 1992, Herman Slotoroff, a retired Somers, New York, accountant, underwent bypass heart surgery. An avid tennis player, Slotoroff was concerned at first that his tennis playing days might be over. During his recuperation, however, he was assured by doctors that along with a good diet, exercise, including tennis, was essential to his recovery.

CHALLENGE

During his recovery, Slotoroff, who was grateful for the expert medical treatment he had received, decided that he wanted to find a way to help raise funds for heart research. In addition, as he had resumed playing tennis just as aggressively as he had before, he wanted to find some way to demonstrate to other heart patients just how important an active exercise program could be to their recovery.

PLAN

A year after his operation, Slotoroff found a way to combine both of his goals—fundraising for heart research and demonstrating the importance of exercise—into a single program. Armed with legal advice and tremendous energy, he formed a nonprofit corporation, the By-Pass Open, to develop his concept. Its purpose was to present an annual round-robin tennis tournament for former heart patients. Players or their sponsors—typically family and friends—would donate at least $100 per player to the American Heart Association. Although he had never organized a public event before, Slotoroff prepared a list of pre-event essentials, printed By-Pass Open stationery, and set out to tackle each aspect of the program. He found a nearby tennis club that agreed to donate its premises on an off day, a Monday, found local caterers to donate food, and wrote and mailed press releases with the pro bono help of a public relations professional. Aided by friends and doctors, he put together a mailing list of recovering heart patients. With his package intact, he was able to win event endorsement from the nearby American Heart Association chapter.

● RESULT

Although the first By-Pass Open, which was held in May 1994, was only a moderate success, it set the stage for future success. Attracting fourteen recovering heart patients as participants, the open netted $4,500 for the American Heart Association. In addition to the round-robin tennis, players were treated to a low-fat pre-event breakfast and post-tournament luncheon and the presentation of winners. Slotoroff himself, with his wife, Elaine, acting as hostess and helper, picked up all the expenses associated with the event. Since that beginning, the By-Pass Open has become an annual fixture, with as many as forty-five players participating. It has attracted players from as far

The Sixth Annual

BY-PASS-OPEN®
TENNIS TOURNAMENT

THE AMERICAN HEART ASSOCIATION
Silver Sponsors: **GEORGE E. REED HEART CENTER**
AT WESTCHESTER MEDICAL CENTER
USTA/EASTERN SECTION

DATE: June 8, 1999 (Rain or Shine)
PLACE: Armonk Tennis Club
Route 22 • Armonk, N.Y.
TIME: 8:30 a.m. to 4:30 p.m.
FORMAT: Round Robin Doubles

MINIMUM PLAYER SPONSORS' DONATION OF $100.00
*PAYABLE TO: **AMERICAN HEART ASSOCIATION***
Complimentary Breakfast, Lunch, Balls, Favors and Prizes

Life is a Participating Activity – Not a Spectator Sport
Life Begins at the **By-Pass Open®**
FOR INFORMATION CALL HERMAN A. SLOTOROFF (914) 666-9288
BY-PASS-OPEN® • Post Office Box 950, Mount Kisco, New York 10549
www.bypassopen.org

The printing of this poster was donated by **THE PLAZA PRINTERS** • 7 Kirby Plaza, Mt. Kisco, NY • 914-666-8888

By-Pass Open Tennis Tournament poster. Reprinted with permission.

away as Seattle and such celebrities as former New York City Mayor David Dinkins. One player, CNN financial news commentator Myron Kandel, was so impressed with the concept that he arranged for CNN to cover it as a news special. During its first six years, the By-Pass Open donated over $75,000 to the American Heart Association. In 1999, when it netted $12,500, the event, which was held at the Armonk Tennis Club in Armonk, New York, under the slogan, "Life is a participating activity, not a spectator sport," was tied into the qualifying tournament for the prestigious Citibank Champions.

QUESTIONS TO ASK

1. Have you explored every step needed to make the dream become a reality?

2. Have you recruited all the volunteer support that may be available to you?

3. Are you prepared, if necessary, to bear the entire financial burden of putting a new program together?

LESSONS LEARNED

Commitment to a concept—combined with energy, common sense, and a professional approach—can be a powerful motivational force. Under the right conditions, it can even make something happen that never happened before.

LAST WORD

If somebody doesn't get the ball rolling, it will remain in the same place.

Whatever You Do, Don't Ask for Money

Requesting In-Kind Support

BACKGROUND

Bratislava Conservatory, in the capital of Slovakia, was founded in 1919, the same year Slovakia and the Czech Republic merged to form Czechoslovakia (the union was dissolved at the end of 1992). Over the years, the conservatory graduated some five thousand students and won renown because of the success of its music, dance, and theater graduates, who were acclaimed as the best representatives of Slovakian culture.

○ CHALLENGE

The conservatory was suffering from a serious lack of funds. In an economically depressed city, the potential for finding the revenue it needed for its survival seemed all but impossible. When Patrick Sciarratta, executive director of Friendship Ambassadors Foundation, visited the conservatory in 1995, he was asked by the organization's leaders if he had any funding suggestions. Sciarratta, who had long experience in wrestling with the funding problems of organizations in emerging nations as a result of his agency's work in promoting global cooperation through cultural exchange, suggested an unusual strategy. "Why not," he asked, "launch a local campaign built around the theme, 'We don't want your money?' Ask for in-kind support instead."

◑ PLAN

Conservatory officials immediately picked up the concept of promoting and marketing a program based on in-kind support rather than contributions. As the plan developed, the "We don't want your money" headline appeared on fliers that were distributed to local businesses and professionals, who were asked to contribute goods or services in return for tickets to performances.

● RESULT

The concept captured the imagination of the community and won immediate support for the conservatory. One doctor, in return for two concert subscriptions, treated conservatory students with colds without charge. A local baker gave bread to dormitory residents in return for a subscription. The six-month-long campaign brought the conservatory the immediate support it needed. The services that were provided allowed the institution to free up the cash that it might have spent on such services and to use it for other needs. The campaign served a second important purpose. It helped engender a closer relationship between the conservatory and local citizens and set the stage for actual funding later.

QUESTIONS TO ASK

1. Have you thoroughly explored which funding endeav-
    ors are most suitable to the audience you will solicit?

2. Have you explored how you can use in-kind support as
    a jumping-off point for funding from other sources?

3. How do you best promote an unusual concept?

LESSONS LEARNED

Base your funding campaign on a reasonable expectation
of what your target audience can afford to give, not on what
tradition dictates.

LAST WORD

In-kind can be most kind, when you really need it.

Fathering Your Nest

Involving Target Audiences

BACKGROUND

The Somers Library in Somers, New York, is a small library in a northern Westchester County community of under twenty thousand. Located in a parklike setting, with recreational facilities nearby, it was founded as a free association library in 1957 and become the free public library of the town in 1981. It is a heavily used facility, with eleven thousand cardholders. The library more than doubled its space in 1993 through an expansion project that created new program and reading rooms. In 1999, a three-year expansion of its children's area, the site for a range of popular programs, was completed.

○ CHALLENGE

Although the children's division of the library has been successful in drawing mothers and their young children to its activities, the library faced a problem fairly common to programs aimed at children and their parents—the absence of fathers. Children's librarian Maureen Tine decided that an attractive program designed specifically to involve children and their dads in a quality-time activity could be a vehicle to attract fathers to the library.

◑ PLAN

Recognizing that a male viewpoint was needed to help develop such a program, Tine turned to library volunteer Gregg Fonde, a Somers resident and middle school teacher in nearby Eastchester. Putting their heads together, they came up with a concept for the first Dad's Day for youngsters in grades two to five and their fathers—a storytelling hour led by Gregg, followed by the playing of board games, a fun activity designed to involve fathers with their children. Once the program details were worked out, Tine received approval to promote the event and spend up to $100 on board games, which, with shrewd shopping at discount stores, resulted in the purchase of some twenty-five games. Posters were put up at the library, notices were included in the library's monthly calendar, and fliers were sent to area schools announcing the program. Designed as an icebreaker, the event was intended to draw a handful of dads and then build on that number in succeeding events.

● RESULT

The first Dad's Day program was held on April 24, 1999, with competition from soccer and other activities. It exceeded expectations, with twelve dads and their kids attending. To involve fathers and children in storytelling, Gregg told some stories and then invited the youngsters to pick up any book in the library, select a picture from it, and then make up a story around that picture with the help of their fathers, if needed. The games session that followed, which included the introduction by Gregg of a game new to everyone, an Egyptian checkers-style game, was especially successful. All of the fathers, including several who had approached the event with a decided lack of

DAD'S DAY

A Father and child
Storytelling & Activity Hour

Storyteller, Gregg Fonde, is a Somers resident and an Eastchester Middle School Teacher.

SAT., MAY 22 1999

10:30 -11:30 a.m.
Grades 2-5
No age requirements
for the fathers!

Fathers and children, wear your
favorite thinking caps (hats).

Somers Library Program Room
REGISTRATION REQUIRED
(914) 232-5717

Dad's Day flier from event held by Somers Library. Reprinted with permission.

enthusiasm, admitted to enjoying themselves. The library has since made Dad's Day an ongoing program.

QUESTIONS TO ASK

1. To reach a target audience, can someone who speaks that audience's language help you?

2. Are you prepared to start small if there's potential for growth?

3. Have you targeted a target audience?

LESSONS LEARNED

If you've had difficulty in reaching a key audience, enlist a peer member of that group, develop a small concept that you can handle easily, and enlist all the promotional help you can to reach that audience.

LAST WORD

An icebreaker can lead you to smooth sailing ahead.

Reading the Riot Act

Developing Programs Through Grassroots Involvement

BACKGROUND

Bronx Educational Services runs an adult literacy program in the South Bronx, New York. A group of its adult literacy students were concerned about their own reading deficiencies and even more concerned by the low reading scores for the neighborhood schools that their children and friends' children attended. A field trip for parents and children to a fourth-grade classroom was arranged, with the aim of convincing the children to stay in school so that they would not have to take remedial courses or go back to school as adults. But the parents on the trip became angered and upset when they saw that students were receiving scant attention from their teachers. They voiced their concern to the leaders of Bronx Educational Services.

○ CHALLENGE

Program leaders, set to receive funding from the Edna McConnell Clark Foundation, decided that a new opportunity had presented itself. They decided to submit a proposal to the foundation to fund a project in which the literacy students would play a key role—organizing parents in a single public school, P.S. 62 in the Bronx—in helping improve reading quality.

◑ PLAN

The Parent Organization and Education Project of Bronx Educational Services, funded by the foundation, involved parents as participants through the organization of a parents committee and a door-to-door campaign. Parents learned how to present the problem of how to improve reading quality in the schools to other parents and were motivated to attend school board meetings and voice their concerns in public.

● RESULT

Two years after the project was started, its organizers decided that it was important enough to go out on its own. Under its new name, Mothers on the Move, the group expanded its involvement to other neighborhood schools that had problems similar to those facing P.S. 62. They also broadened the program to focus on other neighborhood issues, such as tenant rights, crime, environmental issues, and traffic safety. Along the way, the group, with some seven hundred moms and several dads, has picked up additional private foundation support to conduct training seminars and provide technical assistance to parents and parent groups from other communities. The many tangible results that have been realized include getting mothers on the school board, removing an entrenched school superintendent who had battled progressive moves, and helping tenants win rent relief.

QUESTIONS TO ASK

1. Is there an issue that can be identified?

2. Is there a group of people who can be organized around the issue?

3. What resources are available?

LESSONS LEARNED

You can motivate people to become involved in an issue that directly affects them, regardless of their background, and if they're sufficiently motivated and properly trained, they can become very effective advocates.

LAST WORD

The soil is often fertile under the grass roots, but it must be cultivated before anything can grow.

AFTERWORD

YEARS AGO, when I was making guest appearances on radio and television shows to promote an early book of mine, *Culture and Company,* I noticed a similarity in the questions asked by several of the celebrities who hosted talk shows that I didn't notice among the less celebrated but decidedly more cerebral hosts. Among the former, virtually all the questions and comments were restricted to material that appeared in the first two or three chapters of the book. Perhaps, I thought, I should have inserted a note on a page near the end of the book, offering a cash reward to anyone who had read that far.

In the case of this book, I can only hope that anyone who has read this far doesn't need a cash reward. I hope instead that reading the cases of nonprofit organizations that have persevered in their efforts to reach the goals set for themselves and have met those goals despite many challenges, may be reward enough. For these organizations are coauthors of this book and the examples they have set may, in microcosm, reflect the examples set by thousands of organizations in every area of the nonprofit world virtually every day of the week.

List of Profiled Organizations